T0358368

.

Mr SIA
Fly Past

Foreword by **JY Pillay**

Mr SIA
Fly Past

by
Ken Hickson

 **World Scientific**

NEW JERSEY · LONDON · SINGAPORE · BEIJING · SHANGHAI · HONG KONG · TAIPEI · CHENNAI

Published by

World Scientific Publishing Co. Pte. Ltd.
5 Toh Tuck Link, Singapore 596224
USA office: 27 Warren Street, Suite 401-402, Hackensack, NJ 07601
UK office: 57 Shelton Street, Covent Garden, London WC2H 9HE

Library of Congress Control Number: 2014952574

British Library Cataloguing-in-Publication Data
A catalogue record for this book is available from the British Library.

Profile photos of Mr Lim Chin Beng for the cover provided by Singapore Press Holdings and The Ascott/CapitaLand.

Front cover 747 image from Singapore Airlines.

MR SIA
Fly Past

ISBN 978-981-4596-44-2

Typeset by Stallion Press
Email: enquiries@stallionpress.com

Printed in Singapore

To Winnie Lim

Lim Chin Beng, with his wife Winnie, when he was conferred the highest civilian honour by the Emperor of Japan in 2004 — the Grand Cordon of the Order of the Rising Sun. Winnie passed away in March 2013. (Photo from the Lim family collection.)

FOREWORD

When Ken Hickson asked me to write a foreword to his book on Lim Chin Beng, I accepted with alacrity. Chin Beng was a trusted colleague and friend of mine for decades in the airline industry. Contributing a foreword was the least I could do to anchor the memory of his achievements in the annals of Singapore Airlines.

It is no exaggeration to assert that Chin Beng was a seminal personality in the growth and blossoming of the carrier. He joined the legacy carrier of SIA, known then as Malayan Airways in 1960 and later Malaysia-Singapore Airlines. In 1971, still in his 30s, he took over the reins of MSA as Managing Director.

That was an era of great and continual change, and some turmoil, in the legacy carrier. Over a period of years in the 1960s, the two governments of Malaysia and Singapore periodically raised their stake, *pari passu*, in the joint carrier until they were the dominant shareholders, displacing the private shareholders, which included BOAC and Qantas. Those private owners founded the legacy airline in 1947, and moulded it into a professional carrier, grounded in the basic disciplines of flight operations and engineering maintenance, and offering renowned service in the air and on the ground. Over time, each government evolved its specific strategy for the future of the carrier. That divergence in outlook eventually led to the peaceful break-up of MSA, in October 1972, into two wholly-owned government carriers: Malaysian Airlines System (MAS) and Singapore Airlines (SIA). Lim Chin Beng continued as the CEO of SIA.

Although expectations by the *cognoscenti* were, for understandable reason, modest for the new carrier, Chin Beng and his team were undaunted. Even before SIA took to the skies in October 1972, Chin Beng, with the blessing of the SIA Board, had placed an order for the mighty Jumbo jet or B747. Hardly a year from SIA's launch, the Jumbo started service. The rest, as the weather-beaten phrase goes, is history, which Ken Hickson has professionally and comprehensively depicted in his book.

The interesting question, often asked, is how that fledgling carrier managed to overcome scepticism and systematically climb its way into the top ranks. Observers have quite often pointed out that the people at SIA did not, and do not, look like supermen. Yet they have consistently achieved outstanding results. What is the crucial ingredient?

It is a function of leadership and steady management applied rigorously, fairly and consistently. There was no pompous, airy-fairy vision thing. But there was a passionate dedication to a very high standard and quality of service and a deep commitment to the integrity of the product.

In the early days there were other factors no doubt that favoured SIA. At a time when most airlines were government-owned and heavily subsidised, SIA had to learn to go it alone. It mastered the discipline of flying solo, and was incentivised to take bold but calculated risks. Other carriers in the region may have been pusillanimous about rapid expansion, ordering wide-body jets, and keeping their fleets young, productive, ship-shape and appealing to the customer. Not SIA, which shot ahead of the competition and has substantially retained its ability to innovate.

It is noteworthy that the management team and ethos that Chin Beng helped to fashion has produced each of the four home-grown CEOs that succeeded him. They have retained the ability to effectively harness all the factors of production, efficiently and harmoniously, to deliver what the customer wants. As long as that compact, *esprit de corps* and dedication remain, the airline will continue to flourish despite occasional buffeting.

Lim Chin Beng was a key personality in the making of an outstanding airline. It is right and just that this comprehensive and very readable book by Ken Hickson is now coming out to record, commemorate and celebrate his outstanding contribution to SIA.

JY Pillay
September 2014

FOREWORD

As a relatively junior manager, I had the privilege of attending meetings led by Mr Lim and learning from the example he set, especially in negotiations for bilateral air traffic rights and for the purchases of aircraft.

He always held pre-meetings with the support staff and prepared himself well. At the actual negotiations, the things that impressed me most were Mr Lim's composure, politeness and pragmatism. As a leader of the executive team, he always gave them credit for success and never blamed them for failure.

Mr Lim mixed well with people socially and was comfortable not only with peers but notably also with subordinates. He has a good sense of humour and a ready repertoire of jokes to suit the occasion.

Apart from being a leader, Mr Lim was a gentleman and diplomat. It was no surprise that as Singapore's Ambassador to Japan, he was instrumental in the successful conclusion of the free trade agreement between the two countries, one of the first moves by Japan towards trade liberalisation.

Chew Choon Seng
October 2014

Mr Chew followed in Lim Chin Beng's footsteps at two major Singapore institutions. He was CEO of Singapore Airlines from 2003 to 2010 and started with the airline the year it was launched (1971). He is currently Chairman of the Singapore Tourism Board (STB) and Chairman of the Singapore Exchange (SGX).

CONTENTS

LIM CHIN BENG:
HIS STORY AT A GLANCE

1932 Born in Bandung, Indonesia, where his father was an English teacher, on 28 September.

1946 Along with parents and siblings, bundled into a British DC3, evacuated from Bandung and taken to Penang.

1948 Family moved to Singapore and he enrolled as a student at Raffles Institution.

1951 Enrolled at University of Malaya in Singapore (which was later to be renamed National University of Singapore) to study Economics, Mathematics and Statistics.

1956 Graduated with BA (Honours) in Economics, Class II Upper, after obtaining his BA the previous year.

   Joined the Singapore Government Administrative Service in the Ministry of Finance, then called The Treasury.

1960 Joined Malayan Airways in Singapore as an administrative trainee and went on to hold various positions. The airline changed its name to Malaysian Airways in 1963 and Malaysia-Singapore Airlines (MSA) in 1967.

1971 Appointed Deputy Managing Director of Malaysia-Singapore Airlines (MSA) effective 1 January and Managing Director, effective 26 July.

1972	First Managing Director of Singapore Airlines when it launched in October that year. He remained in the post for 10 years.
	Completed an Advanced Management Programme at Harvard Business School.
1982	First Deputy Chairman of Singapore Airlines, a Board position he held until 1996.
1985	Named Chairman of the Singapore Tourist Promotion Board, as it was called then, and remained there until 1989.
1986	Won the Singapore Businessman of the Year Award.
1990	Given the Outstanding Contribution to Tourism Award.
1991	Appointed Singapore's Ambassador to Japan. He served two terms, returning to Singapore in 1997.
1993	On hand at Changi Airport on 12 October to take delivery of the 1000th 747 aircraft produced by Boeing.
1997	Appointed member of the Singapore Public Service Commission, on which he served until 2008.
1998	Inducted into the International Aviation Laureates Hall of Fame by Aviation Week and Space Technology.
	Chairman of Singapore Technologies Aerospace, a position he held for six years until 2005.
	Chairman of Asian Aerospace.
	Became a member of the Singapore Legal Service Commission, where he continued to serve until 2007.
	Appointed a Director of three Singapore companies: Pontiac Land, CapitaLand and Star Hub.
2000	Chairman of The Ascott Limited, which he held until 2012.
2001	Chief Negotiator for the Singapore/Japan Free Trade Agreement (signed in 2002).
	Made a Director of Singapore Press Holdings.
2002	Elected Chairman of Singapore Press Holdings, a position he held until 2005.
2003	Chairman of Valuair Limited, a company he established to launch Singapore's first low cost carrier in 2004.
	Co-leader of the Singapore/India Joint Study Group to conclude a Free Trade Agreement.

2004	Conferred the Grand Cordon of the Order of the Rising Sun by the Emperor of Japan.
2005	Chairman of Singapore Airshow and Events Ltd, until 2009.
	Chairman of CapitaLand Hope Foundation, through to 2012.
2007	Chairman of Changi Airports International, a position he held until 2012.
	Awarded Public Service Star.
2012– Present	Retired from all directorships.

Arrived in Style: Lim Chin Beng, wife Winnie (left) and daughter Sharon (right) accompanied by four Singapore Girls at the steps of the 1000th 747 produced by Boeing in 1993 when SIA was chosen for this special delivery. (Photo from the Lim family collection.)

"All the world's a stage, and all the men and women merely players:
they have their exits and their entrances;
and one man in his time plays many parts,
his acts being seven ages".

(William Shakespeare, *As You Like It*)

CHAPTER 1

DELIVERY TIMES

The man who signed on the dotted line for Singapore Airlines (SIA) for its very first order of two Boeing 747s in 1972 was the very same person on the spot to take delivery 21 years later of the 1000th jumbo jet produced by the world's largest aircraft manufacturer.

It was on 12 October 1993, when Lim Chin Beng, the Deputy Chairman of the airline which was that year — and for many other years — voted the world's best airline, was in the limelight and sharing the stage with Phil Condit, the President of Boeing Aircraft Company.

At the time Mr Lim was quoted as saying: "Singapore Airlines and its 12,000 employees worldwide are honoured to be part of aviation history". He went on to mention the airline's long term and mutually beneficial relationship with Boeing "exemplified by the delivery of this landmark aircraft"[1].

But for Mr Lim — the man charged with managing the fledging airline which evolved out of Malaysia-Singapore Airlines (MSA) and before that Malayan Airways — SIA might not have taken to Boeing like a duck to water.

It was among the number of bold moves taken by Mr Lim, as the first Managing Director of SIA, in the months following the decision by the Governments of Singapore and Malaysia to "go their own way" in the airline business.

But like most management decisions, they were not taken lightly. Before the dotted line was signed to commit to buy 747s in 1972, the airline had conducted an extremely thorough evaluation of three wide-bodied jet types on offer from three different manufacturers at the time. Besides the Boeing jumbo, there was the McDonnell Douglas DC-10 and the Lockheed L-1011. Mr Lim was convinced that the best choice for the airline was the Boeing option, which was also the biggest and most expensive of the three.

Mr Lim had been an airline man for 12 years when he was — as he describes it — the "most senior Singaporean" in the management ranks and given the job of running the new airline. Besides his experience working under airline "bosses" who hailed from United Kingdom and Australia in Malayan Airways and MSA, he also had a degree in economics, mathematics and statistics behind him, and somehow he managed to fit in an Advanced Management Programme at Harvard in the year of 1972, when SIA came into its own.

So when he was there to take delivery of Boeing's 1000th 747 in 1993, Mr Lim was a very seasoned airline man and was holding onto his Deputy Chairman's position on top of his day job, which was at the time Singapore's Ambassador to Japan. In fact, the only company directorship he was allowed to maintain during his two terms (from 1991 to 1997) as a diplomat in the Ministry of Foreign Affairs, based in Tokyo, was his SIA role.

He also had to tread something of a diplomatic tight rope when Boeing drew attention to the fact that "only two airlines in the world, Japan Airlines and British Airways, have received more" 747s than SIA.

As Boeing notes in its report of that significant delivery job, "the new super jet will be Singapore's 55th 747".

Boeing could hardly contain itself on this occasion and pointed out to media — it had assembled news representatives from 12 countries to record the event — that with this delivery, SIA will have received since 1973, 69 Boeing jetliners (including 727s and 757s) valued at about US$5.2 billion.

Boeing also noted that with "twenty additional 747s on order and options for 15 more, if exercised, will bring SIA's 747 purchases to 104 airplanes worth an estimated US$10.6 billion".

What Boeing apparently did not include that day in its aircraft tally was that three Boeing 707s and five 737s were "inherited" from MSA in 1972.

What was all important to Boeing and SIA was this one VIP — "very important plane" — and as one of the other visiting VIPs on the spot, Boeing's Mr Condit put it: "We take exceptional pride that Singapore Airlines, whose fleet of 747s has become a signature at the airports of nearly every major world capital, will receive this milestone jetliner".

It was one particular aircraft which had special endorsement from an even higher office.

When the 1000th jumbo emerged four weeks earlier from Boeing's plant — described as the world's largest building — and before entering a month of flight testing and final preparation, United States President Bill Clinton sent word[2]:

> I would like to congratulate all of you on the completion of the 1000th Boeing 747. It is a testament to the ingenuity and hard work of the American people. In an increasingly competitive marketplace, you can take great pride in your ability to grow and prosper.

What the President did not say, but Boeing was quick to point out, was that 747 sales at that stage (October 1993) had totalled US$141.8 billion since Pan Am received the very first jumbo in 1969. Another US$28.4 billion of announced 747-400s remained on order.

The mention of Pan Am in this context must have made some aviation scribes sit up and take note that here was SIA, considered by some as an "upstart" international airline, taking delivery of this 1000th 747, when the airline that took delivery of its first jumbo 24 years previously had unceremoniously gone out of business two years before Boeing produced this "commemorative edition".

The pioneering Pan American World Airways, commonly known as Pan Am and described in its prime as "the world's most experienced airline", was the principal and largest international air carrier in the United States from 1927 until its collapse on 4 December 1991.

But it was SIA's day as far as Boeing was concerned and an opportunity for Boeing in its press announcement to set out its latest statistics, which showed that the worldwide fleet of 747s for all airlines had flown more than 1.4 billion passengers — roughly a quarter of the Earth's population — a distance equal to 80,000 trips to the moon.

Its latest model, Boeing pointed out, the 747-400 flies 8,290 miles (13,340km) non-stop. Its engine noise was half of what it was on the original jumbos delivered in early 1970s. Its modern digital flight deck means a smaller number of crew required to fly it, making it the most efficient jetliner in production on a seat-mile cost basis.

It was also left to Boeing — though SIA was very proud to proclaim the delivery as an honour for the nation and its airline — that "while the airline last December (1992) celebrated 20 years of service with 747s, SIA's policy of fleet renewal ensures that passengers fly on the most comfortable, efficient and reliable aircraft available". At an average age of just over five years, SIA's passenger fleet at the time was among the youngest and most modern of the world's major airlines.

As a matter of record, in October 1993, the airline's profitability was duly acknowledged by the aircraft supplier. SIA enjoyed an after-tax profit of US$548 million on 1992/93 revenues of US$3.4 billion (fiscal year ending March 31), which was up 4.2% over the previous year. This was put down to an increase in capacity as the carrier boosted the frequency of services to Asia, Europe, the Americas and South-West Pacific.

New destinations inaugurated in 1992 had included New York, Madrid, Hanoi and Durban, giving SIA a route network spanning 70 cities in 40 countries.

It was not Mr Lim who drew attention to these "success factors" but it was set out for all to see in the official media release from Boeing. On this auspicious occasion, when the traditional lion dance noisily competed with the whir of jet engines, he would have all these facts and figures — and more — in his head. But he never let occasions like this to "go to his head".

Ever the modest diplomat and airline industry leader — inducted into the "Laureates of Fame" by the Aviation Week and Space Technology Magazine in 1998 — he took these events in his stride.

He was quick to point out, if a journalist chose to draw attention to his achievements in making SIA so successful, that the airline had a great team of people. It took collective effort and teamwork. Even when he was honoured with the title "Businessman of the Year" in Singapore 1986, and his oil portrait was unveiled in front of Government and business leaders, he had arranged for a group of SIA stewardesses, along with airline operation staff, to get in the picture and share the limelight.

So typical of this man they called "Mr SIA" to share the credit for his own achievements and that of the airline he managed. This is also evident in the photograph of the "acceptance" of the 1000th 747, where four uniformed Singapore Girls are on the arrival steps behind Mr Lim, his wife Winnie and their daughter Sharon.

While the "airline family" and his own family shared the limelight here, he always made it his practice to include family members in his business life and his travels.

He gives credit to his dear wife Winnie (who sadly passed away in March 2013) for being his partner while he served at the Singapore Mission in Tokyo. She was responsible for single-handedly influencing some important events — largely through her "golf diplomacy" — and led Mr Lim to recommend a greater role for spouses as they "can play a very supportive and important role for the diplomats".

His daughter Sharon came in for special attention, when he was interviewed in 2001 and was asked whether his children were following his example by taking career risks and maintaining a broader range of interests. He advocated that one should "be strong in your specialisation" but also strive to be a "generalist" and have a range of other interests.

After working as a neurologist for 10 years, Sharon decided to broaden her education and enrolled in an MBA course at London Business School, opening up "new avenues of opportunities", beyond her professional medical qualifications, Mr Lim said at the time.

Son Arthur, while he did not follow in his father's footsteps into Singapore Airlines, focussing instead on the hotel and tourism industry, but he did join forces with the senior Mr Lim in the Valuair venture to set up Singapore's first privately-owned budget airline, taking on the important role of director covering operations and customer services.

Setting examples for his family and staff — in leadership, in business, in diplomacy, in taking on a broad range of interests — has been typical of Mr Lim. As the story of "Mr SIA" clearly shows, this is a man of many parts or as Shakespeare wrote:

All the world's a stage, and all the men and women merely players: they have their exits and their entrances; and one man in his time plays many parts, his acts being seven ages.

Lim Chin Beng has shown he can play many parts — on the world's stage and at home — not as a bit player, but as a reluctant star performer. And as the recounting of his life and work to date clearly demonstrates his "acts" cover at least seven ages: airline industry leader, economist, diplomat, businessman of the year, chairman (deputy chairman and director) of many organisations, dedicated husband and father, and real gentleman.

That day in October 1993, when he was on hand to accept an important delivery of a very significant big jet, also turned out to be an occasion when he unwittingly demonstrated that he was "playing many parts" typical of his days and years before and those still to come.

Endnotes

1. 1000th Boeing 747 delivering to Singapore Airlines (11 October 1993), PR Newswire for Boeing Company. Available at http://www.thefreelibrary.com/1%2c000TH+BOEING +747+DELIVERING+TO+SINGAPORE+AIRLINES-a014227961.

2. Mr Clinton is quoted in the Boeing media release issued on the day.

Good Sports: The young Lim Chin Beng (far right, top row) in the 1950 volleyball team while a student at Raffles Institution, where he also excelled at basketball and in music.
(Raffles Institution photo.)

"Nurturing thinkers, leaders and pioneers of character
who serve by leading and lead in serving."

(The mission statement of Raffles Institution, founded by Sir Stamford Raffles
in 1823 and attended by Lim Chin Beng from 1948 for three years.)

CHAPTER 2

RAFFLES INSPIRED

For someone who was born in Indonesia, went to school in Penang (Malaysia), was a British subject, became a graduate of the University of Malaya, and left the Singapore civil service to work as a management trainee at Malayan Airways, the young Lim Chin Beng could be forgiven if he suffered from a national identity crisis.

For the record, he is happy to admit that he was born in Bandung, Indonesia on 28 September 1932, where his father, originally from Penang, was teaching English. He started out at "my father's school" as it was one of the few English schools in Indonesia at that time.

He recalls the war time in Indonesia as "not as hard as what I read it to be in Malaysia and Singapore". As there was no resistance to the Japanese invasion, there was no retaliation against the population. Indonesia, as he pointed out at the time, was such a rich country and no shortage of food.

He has maintained a good relationship with his birth country, even though when he left with his parents, brothers and sisters, they were all pleased to get away from a place which had gone through Japanese occupation, Dutch colonial management and about to experience a revolution which eventually gave the Indonesians their own country[1].

As a child he did not fully understand what was going on when he, along with brothers and sisters, were bundled into a British Royal Air Force DC3 and taken to Jakarta and eventually to Penang in 1946, where they could remain British subjects and not be forced to be citizens in Dutch-run, Indonesia.

As his parents were originally from Penang, the young Lim had two years schooling there, before his father decided that Singapore was the place to be, as he saw more opportunities for his children there. They became Singapore citizens in 1948, while the country was still under British rule.

He described his experience quite graphically in an Oral History interview[2]:

> *After the war, the Japanese gave the Indonesians independence. But when the Dutch came back, the Dutch did not recognise the independence, so there was what we call, the Indonesian revolution. And because my parents were from Penang, I was born a British subject, not as a Dutch or Indonesian subject, but British. So we were evacuated by the British Army in 1946 back to Penang.*
>
> *I was 14 (in 1946) and I stayed in Penang for a couple of years. Again my father decided that Singapore had better prospect than Penang, so the whole family moved down to Singapore in 1948.*

A chapter in the book *100 Inspiring Rafflesians*, about alumni of the notable Raffles Institution in Singapore, is headed "Reach for the Sky" and notes in the first line that "Lim Chin Beng is popularly known as 'Mr SIA'". Over three pages, the chapter makes this reference to his early days[3].

> *Lim studied at St Xaviers Institution and the Penang Free School. When his parents moved to Singapore (in 1948) he was admitted to Raffles Institution.*

When he attended Raffles Institution it was located in Bras Basah Road, where Raffles City now is and opposite Raffles Hotel. He used to travel to school from his home in Katong by tram.

Later in life, he is prepared to admit he did not excel at school — he had to sit his O-levels twice and failed his Chinese one year — but he persevered.

As he decided on an English education as distinct from being Chinese-educated — probably as much as anything because his father was a teacher of English — this penalised him somewhat on the job front later, working as a civil servant in the newly independent Singapore. But it turned out to be a blessing in disguise as it eventually made him turn to the private sector and into the airline business. He put it this way[4]:

> *At the time there happened to be an advertisement in the news-papers for a trainee for Malayan Airways. And I took a pay cut and joined as a trainee in Malayan Airways.*

Before he became a civil servant, he studied at the University of Malaya, which evolved from the merger of Raffles College and the King Edward VII College of Medicine in October 1949. The two institutions were merged to provide for the higher education needs of the Federation of Malaya and Singapore. The young Lim graduated in 1955 with a Bachelor of Arts (Economics, Mathematics and Statistics) and a year later added an Honours in Economics (Upper Second Class)[5].

His job in the Ministry of Finance was not that humdrum. He recalls that at the time The Treasury — as it was called — was run by Mr Tom Hart and he told the young Lim Chin Beng on his first day that he had come to work in "the most important department in the whole Government". It made him take his job very seriously. One of his jobs at a time was to be clerk of the Income Tax Board of Review[6].

He points out that when he joined Malayan Airways as an administrative trainee he had to take a 10% salary cut from his Government job: "I was more interested in a different office culture, where there were fewer regulations and bureaucracy. I was keen to see the results of my work immediately"[7].

It wasn't because he had a burning ambition to join the important new aviation industry or that he had a love of planes. The early grounding in the "plane" business for the man who was to become "Mr SIA" was a different story.

> *It also coincided with the Malayan Airways policy of Malayani-sation. So the moral of the story is — don't worry about the short*

term, even if you get a salary cut. The long term outlook is more important. You should follow your own interests[8].

The majority of the shareholders of the new airline were from Australia (Qantas) and British Overseas Airways Corporation (BOAC), which later became British Airways. "There was already, at the time I joined, some pressure for them to have some local men in the top management of the airline, so they created this position of administrative trainee".

He was fortunate to have good mentors. He was one of only two management trainees, but the other formerly with the Immigration Department, did not last the distance. So it was over to the young Lim to be the pioneering local manager in the airline. He gives full credit to the expatriate bosses for the encouragement they gave him.

Learning along the way from foreigners — British and Australian — who had loads of airline industry experience. He also kept his feet on the ground — when he wasn't flying — but seemed to be in the right place at the right time. A young man with an aptitude for numbers — an economics graduate remember — and someone who quickly learned the ropes and was mentored well by the likes of Charles Spurrell, Roger Mollard and Keith Hamilton.

In the past he had gone through various airline functions — reservations, night duty at airport — all good preparation for what was to come. On 16 September 1963, the Federation of Malaysia was born and the airline became known as Malaysian Airways Limited. He was made Director of Administration.

After five years with the airline based in Raffles Place, Singapore, he was then given his first overseas post to Jesselton — now Kota Kinabalu — and the capital of the state of Sabah, located in East Malaysia.

He recalls that his first overseas appointment was when Malaysian Airways decided to buy over Borneo Airways and he was sent to be Area Manager, looking after the whole area. It was an important post as air transportation was becoming very important in the area. It would take about 30 minutes to fly by light aircraft between some areas, but many days to walk through the jungle as well as trek up and down mountains.

He remembered that DC3s would operate the service from Singapore to Kuching and Sibu, then onto Bintulu, Labuan and Jesselton.

There were challenges he faced at that time, representing the airline in a remote, but important location, with the shortage of good people and limited airport facilities.

Things got better, he says, many years later, when Malaysian Airways introduced the Comet 4 between Singapore and Jesselton.

He recalls being in his home in Jesselton, hearing the reverse thrust of the jet engine of the Comet. "I would jump in my car and go to the airport to collect my newspapers".

It wasn't long before he was recalled to Singapore and more change was in the air. He was made assistant to the airline's General Manager (Keith Hamilton).

He was also given some good training. He even had a trip to the United Kingdom to be attached, first to BOAC, then BEA — British European Airways, which was a division of BOAC — and then six months in Ireland with Aer Lingus.

His job description when he was back in Singapore involved budgeting for the airline, evaluating new aircraft and doing an economic assessment of new routes.

In May 1966, it became Malaysia-Singapore Airlines (MSA), with equal shareholding between Singapore and Malaysia. History records that in 1968, for the first time, the airline's annual revenue hit S$100 million. The *sarong kebaya* uniform for the Singapore Girl, designed by French couturier Pierre Balmain, was introduced and three B707s were added to the fleet. In 1969, the airline purchased five B737-100s[9].

Lim Chin Beng was in the thick of this while serving as right hand man to the boss — he was assistant to the General Manager Keith Hamilton, who eventually went back to Qantas in Australia — and he was made Deputy Managing Director of MSA in January 1971. By July, he was promoted to Managing Director. This was in preparation for the eventual parting of the ways and the official move to make it Singapore Airlines in October 1972.

The journey from his birthplace in Bandung, Indonesia took him to many places and through many experiences — study, work and play — but time and time again he seemed to be in the right place at the right time.

As he modestly puts it when asked how he felt at the time when he was made SIA's first Managing Director in 1972: "I suppose I was the most senior Singaporean on the management team on hand".

Endnotes

1. The Japanese invasion and subsequent occupation in 1942–45 during WWII ended Dutch rule, and encouraged the previously suppressed Indonesian independence movement. Two days after the surrender of Japan in August 1945, nationalist leader, Sukarno, declared independence and became president. The Netherlands tried to re-establish its rule, but a bitter armed and diplomatic struggle ended in December 1949, when in the face of international pressure, the Dutch formally recognised Indonesian independence. From http://en.wikipedia.org/wiki/History_of_Indonesia

2. From transcript of Interview with Patricia Lee for National Archives Oral History Section in the year 2000, available at www.nas.gov.sg/archivesonline/oral_history_interviews. Henceforth, referred to as Mr Lim's National Archives interview.

3. From *100 Inspiring Rafflesians, 1823–2003*, by Guan Heng Tan (World Scientific, 2007).

4. From Mr Lim's National Archives interview.

5. In 1960, the governments of the then Federation of Malaya and Singapore indicated their desire to change the status of the divisions into that of a national university and legislation was passed in 1961 establishing the former Kuala Lumpur division as the University of Malaya while the Singapore division was renamed the University of Singapore on 1 January 1962. It became the National University of Singapore in 1980. Taken from the history of the National University of Singapore, available at http://www.nus.edu.sg/identity/evolution.php.

6. From Mr Lim's National Archives interview.

7. From *100 Inspiring Rafflesians, 1823–2003*, by Guan Heng Tan (World Scientific, 2007).

8. From *100 Inspiring Rafflesians*.

9. That MSA had annual revenue of S$100 million by 1968 recorded by Justin Corfield in the *Historical Dictionary of Singapore* (Scarecrow Press, 2010).

Fitting Design: Miss See Biew Wah, training and check stewardess with Singapore Airlines (SIA) getting a fitting for the Sarong Kebaya from French designer Pierre Balmain (right) and Mademoiselle Madellene Kohler, left) Balmain's Director of Creations and Special Projects. (From the Singapore Airlines collection.)

"Where do you go to my lovely? When you're alone in your bed,
Tell me the thoughts that surround you, I want to look inside your head,
yes I do.
You talk like Marlene Dietrich, And you dance like Zizi Jeanmaire,
Your clothes are all made by Balmain.
And there's diamonds and pearls in your hair, yes there are".

("Where Do You Go To My Lovely" by Peter Sarstedt, as recorded
on his single released on 5 April 1969.)

CHAPTER 3

DESIGNER DAYS

Everyone knows that Pierre Balmain designed the ever-lasting, enduring uniform of the Singapore Girl. But how did it happen that it was Balmain who got the job and what was his brief?

Lim Chin Beng admits that he was the one to first meet with Monsieur Balmain to give him a briefing for the airline's distinctive uniform.

"He came to meet me in my office in Singapore — the year was 1968 — and I told him what we had in mind. I told him we wanted to use the *sarong kebaya*, the traditional dress for Indonesian and Malaysian women.

The fact that the famous courtier first designed the uniform for the stewardesses of Malaysia-Singapore Airlines, four years before SIA came into being, is often missed.

After walking around the streets of Singapore, the famous French courtier had noted that he could not observe any obvious "culture". To him, says Mr Lim many years later, "nothing stood out".

Mr Balmain took out his pencil and did some rough sketches in Mr Lim's office.

"I said 'that's it', when I saw that he had correctly interpreted the *sarong kebaya*". That sketch became the basic design of the uniform that has lasted for more than 40 years as the iconic look of inflight attendants and a trade mark for SIA.

While the *sarong kebaya* uniform was first introduced to MSA and worn by the flight attendants, it was later developed to become the most prominent symbol of Singapore Airlines' image[1].

When Malaysia-Singapore Airlines ceased operations and Singapore Airlines officially took off on 1 October 1972, the refreshed Singapore Girl's uniform by Pierre Balmain, became the signature and style of the airline. It is regarded as the airline outfit that has lasted longer than any other and it is still winning design and service awards[2].

The *kebaya* is the national costume of Indonesia, although it is more accurately endemic to the Javanese, Sundanese and Balinese peoples. While it is a traditional blouse-dress combination that originates from Indonesia it is often worn by women in Malaysia, Brunei, Burma, Singapore, southern Thailand, and the Southern part of the Philippines.

It is sometimes made from sheer material such as silk, thin cotton or semi-transparent nylon or polyester, adorned with brocade or floral pattern embroidery. *Kebaya* is usually worn with a sarong or *batik kain panjang*, or other traditional woven garment such as *ikat*, *songket* with a colorful motif.

Pierre Balmain is quoted as saying at the time: "I approve of your *sarong kebaya*. I think it is very graceful, and if any alterations are to be made, they should only be to make the dress easier to wear".

He also advised that it should not be worn too tight. "I saw a lovely girl on the plane but she was wearing such a tight sarong that she looked like a mermaid![3]"

Consequently, Balmain insisted that each *kebaya* was individually tailored to fit each stewardess to ensure a feminine fit. Balmain and SIA shared the view that standards set are rigorously adhered to.

The airline expected perfect presentation from the start, and it was something uppermost in the airline chief's mind as he set out to establish SIA as truly an international airline that people would eventually look up to.

To this end, SIA employed a grooming consultant to tailor a make-up colour guide for each employee, to complement her skin tone and features, and uniform fittings are done at least every six months. Besides a minor change to the collar in 1974, Balmain's *sarong kebaya* has remained the same since 1968.

While Balmain based his design on the traditional, he added borders round the hem, neck and cuffs (cut from the edges of the traditional batik fabric) giving it a distinctive appearance and altering the fit for ease of wear. Part of their continual allure is down to Balmain insisting that the uniforms were fully tailored (rather than off the peg), and to this day SIA's in-house tailors have a minimum of two fittings with each crew member and provide her with four new uniforms each year.

In April 2001, the shoes were replaced by Balmain-designed shoes, in light of reviews after the Singapore Airline's Flight 006 crash in Taipei, where flight attendants complained of missing sandals.

There is little doubt in the minds of airline watchers that the ageless appeal of the Singapore Girl is a tribute to Mr Lim's choice and direction of Mr Balmain's creative execution.

Even today, fashion observers like "Crinoline Robot" write about it glowingly:

> *Balmain came up with a slinky, yet covering, batik outfit based on the traditional sarong kebaya. The airline has its staff's uniforms individually fitted every six months to ensure an immaculate fit, and employs grooming consultants to help staff pick the ideal makeup for their colouring.*

She also observed that other airlines may have changed their uniform over the decades, but not Singapore Airlines with its *sarong kebaya*, as it is "elegant and lovely and somehow timeless". Its simplicity of line owes a lot to the 1960s as well as tradition, the fashion observer noted, as the uniform is devoid of pointless frippery, while the classic batik pattern hasn't aged the way many prints would have done.

The Balmain designed uniforms come in four colours that represent the ranking of the Singapore Girls: blue for "Flight Stewardess", green for the "Leading Stewardess", red for "Chief Stewardess", and burgundy for the "In-Flight Supervisor".

When in 1972, Singapore and Malaysia agreed to set up separate airlines by splitting MSA in two (just as Singapore itself gained independence from Malaysia), and the newly formed Singapore Airlines' cabin crew sported the Balmain designed uniforms. It was at this time that the Singapore Girl was born, featuring for the first time in the airline's promotional activity and going on to become an unofficial ambassador for the young island nation and a global icon.

The international Wallpaper magazine noted in a report that the Singapore Girls featured in the advertising campaigns over the past four decades have always been "crew plucked from the aisles, just like Misa and Nursa'adah who flew into Heathrow specially for the magazine photography feature and are never seen dressed in anything else"[5].

Perhaps the ultimate sign of both its longevity and its elegance, the Singapore Girl in Balmain was chosen to feature in Madame Tussauds London in 1993, while Mr Lim was playing the important Deputy Chairman's role for the airline:

Well-known Singapore-based foreign correspondent Michael Richardson at the time — now serving as a research fellow at the Institute of South East Asian Studies — wrote in the International Herald Tribune (9 June 1993)[6]:

> *When the life-size figure of a Singapore Airlines flight attendant is installed this month at Madame Tussauds waxworks in London alongside such other recently arrived celebrities as Presidents Bill Clinton and Saddam Hussein, it will mark a significant broadening of horizons for one of Britain's most popular tourist attraction.*
>
> *With about half its visitors arriving by air from outside Britain, including a growing number from Asia, the wax museum decided to shift its focus a bit.*
>
> *"We felt that as people are traveling more and more by air, we should represent that as well," said Juliet Simkins, head of press and publicity at Madame Tussauds.*

> *Singapore Airlines was chosen, she explained, because it had promoted itself for more than 20 years by using women in the cabin crews to appear as the Singapore Girl in advertising.*

Lim Suet Kwee, who is pictured at the opening of chapter 6, was the flight attendant who sat for the wax sculptors at Madame Tussauds. She was drawn from about 50 of the airline's cabin crew members.

Used to being number one in most airline stakes, it was no shame when in 2013, the Singapore Girl uniform by Pierre Balmain, came in at number two in a very up to date assessment of international airline uniforms.

In the *"The Design Air* Top 10 Airline Uniforms Of 2013", Jonny Clark writes[7]:

> *At The design air we have been watching the recent trend over the past few months of new uniforms being launched around the world, from China Eastern to Virgin Atlantic, new threads have become the new norm, lifting the inflight product and refreshing the cabin look and feel, whilst also (hopefully) making the cabin crew a little bit happier. ...We are happy to announce many of the new uniforms have made it into the Top 10, with some other more classic uniforms showing they have tested time and stayed in our minds-eye as some of the best in the sky. Here's our Top 10 list of good looking uniforms at 35000 ft.*

[Singapore Girl — number 2!]

> *With just a minor tweak in the collar in 1974, Balmain's design, based on the traditional Malay sarong kebaya costume, has been worn by Singapore Airlines flight stewardesses for 39 years. It's a brilliant design: neatly encompassing the requirements of Singapore's multi-cultural, religiously-mixed population.*

[Number one was designed back in 2005 by Gianfranco Ferré for Korean Airlines.]

Choosing the right designer and outfit to set the scene for SIA from the beginning was so important for "the architect" in the hot seat. It was clear in Mr Lim's mind that to be successful in the very competitive international environment, SIA had to stand out.

He thought at the time that Singapore did not have a designer of high enough international standard who could do the job.

"The last thing we wanted was to be seen as an airline from a small Asian island. We needed to be international. This had to come through in the uniforms, the menus, the aircraft livery and the choice of aircraft".

Who could have known that the airline from Singapore which started to take on the world in 1972, would maintain its look and feel for so long and maintain its position more than 40 years later, as a leader in such a competitive global industry?

What a famous French designer and a rookie airline boss cooked up in a Singapore office all that time ago ranks today as the most enduring symbols of success in a cut-throat business, where airlines themselves have risen and collapsed in the same period, not forgetting the cat-walk procession of in-flight uniforms that have come and gone.

The Singapore Girl in her *sarong kebaya* is a lasting testament to bold moves taken by Mr Lim and in line with the other decisions he had to engineer, along with his management team, to get the international look and feel of a world beater of an airline.

Endnotes

1. Wikipedia records that Singapore Girl was coined in 1972 after Pierre Balmain, a French haute couture designer, was originally hired by Malaysia-Singapore Airlines to construct and update the Malay *sarong kebaya* as part of the cabin crew's uniform. Since then, the uniform has gained worldwide recognition as part of SIA's signature branding.

2. Still a name associated with high fashion, Pierre Balmain, the man, passed away in 1982 — ten years after the Singapore Girl emerged as his creation. He studied architecture at the *École des Beaux-Arts*, but did not complete his studies. He spent his time there designing dresses. Balmain then left his architectural studies to work for the fashion designer Edward Molyneux, for whom he worked from 1934 until 1939. He joined Lucien Lelong after World War II and opened his own fashion house in 1945. During the 1950s, Balmain popularised the stole for day as well as evening wear and created a vogue for sheath dresses beneath jackets. His talent as a designer lay in his ability to make simple, tailored suits as well as grand evening gowns, all with the same aesthetic of slender and elegant lines.

3. Quoted in *SIA Takeoff to Success* by Roy Allen (Singapore Airlines Limited, 1990).

4. Magazine journalist by day, "Crinoline Robot" is a blogger on fashion and style, per her take on SIA uniforms (30 October 2013), available at http://crinolinerobot.blogspot.sg/2013/10/the-singapore-girl-and-pierre-balmain.html.

5. Read more at http://www.wallpaper.com/fashion/singapore-airlines-uniform/1638#KIG6XpayVxvaOsxY.99.

6. Article appeared in what was called the *International Herald Tribune* then, but is now *International New York Times*. Still available at http://www.nytimes.com/1993/06/08/style/08iht-wax.html.

7. Report available at http://thedesignair.net/2013/08/04/thedesignair-top-10-airline-uniforms-of-2013/.

Lasting Logos: The logo in black (left) of Singapore Airlines as originally developed by Landor in 1972 which was used until 1987 and the refined in blue and yellow version, updated by Landor and used since 1988. (Logos from Singapore Airlines collection.)

Livery (/ˈliv(ə)ri): A special design and colour scheme used on the vehicles, aircraft, or products of a particular company: the city's trams are painted in a red and white livery.

From Middle English: from Old French livree "delivered", feminine past participle of livrer, from Latin liberare "liberate" (in medieval Latin "hand over"). The original sense was "the dispensing of food, provisions, or clothing to servants"; hence also "allowance of provender for horses", surviving in the phrase at livery and in livery stables. Arose because medieval nobles provided matching clothes to distinguish their servants from others'.

(Taken from Oxford Dictionaries website.)

CHAPTER 4

LIVELY LIVERY

" I left my heart in San Francisco", sang Tony Bennett and it might well have been on Lim Chin Beng's mind when he ventured to San Francisco in early 1972 to see what designers could come up with to make the airline look the part — as a modern, international airline.

Landor Associates, based on a boat in San Francisco Harbour invited Mr Lim and his team to have a look at their ideas for what could be the livery — the look, the branding — of the new airline. More specifically to see how the new Boeing 747s — which SIA was about to purchase — would look like.

As Mr Lim tells it, when he got on board the *Klamath* — the headquarters for branding agency, described as "a forgotten piece of San Francisco history: a gorgeous, hand-built, wooden ferryboat" — the Landor creative people had about 200 design ideas to show him[1].

The big question for Mr Lim that he needed help to answer was "what could or should the new international airline look like?"

Mr Lim says of his livery assessment experience, once he had chosen to work with Walter Landor and his company Landor Associates, whose most recent airline job was the livery for Alitalia, the Italian airline[2]:

> *After a few months, they invited me to go to their office. They said they had some samples to show me. So I went to their office in*

San Francisco, which was on a houseboat. They brought me to a room. I was shocked. [There were] about 200 logos along the wall for me to pick from. So that was a challenge. Anyway we short-listed a few, brought it back, got the board to approve the logo.

Reducing the 200 to 10 "images" was the first challenge. Then Landor came to Singapore with the top ten and presented to the Board of Singapore Airlines.

The choice — which was Mr Lim's favourite — was the distinctive silver *kris*, reinterpreted as a golden bird, on a dark blue tail. The distinctive dark blue and golden stripe alongside the side of the aircraft has remained pretty much the same as it was conceived and selected in 1972.

One significant change has been in the font, case and size of the words "Singapore Airlines" appearing along the length of the aircraft. Of course, the design has to be carefully adapted to suit each different aircraft. First for SIA was the existing 707s and 727s which were switched from MSA logos to the new SIA livery.

For the man who had to "live with the livery" for the new airline, getting the look right from the beginning was very important.

For he had seen the airline go through many transformations — in owner-ship, management, name and branding — from Malayan Airways, when he first joined in 1960, with a not-so-distinctive "flying tiger" on its tail, to a non-descript Malaysian Airways with an even smaller logo, to MSA, with very prominent capital initials on the tail and a small stylised winged tiger.

There was little doubt in Mr Lim's mind that Landor was the man and the design company to go with. At the time, though, he had not seen the historic video which captures the magic of the man and provides a glimpse inside one of the most unusual office settings around.

It shows Walter Landor sitting on the deck of the *Klamath* ferryboat with the San Francisco Bay in the background, where he talks about the art of branding, working with clients, and even a little about himself[3].

For Mr Lim, it was unusual for a business to be based on a boat, but he remembered years later that Richard Branson, the founder of Virgin Airlines, also had his business on a narrow boat on the Thames in London for a time.

He could not help thinking that once you got your bearings, the creative advantages of the boat were undeniable. Advantages like holding client meetings as a gentle breeze played through the conference room.

As the fame of the floating agency spread, people came to understand the deeper significance of Walter's move. It was about freedom, and expression, and freedom of expression. It was about recognising value that no one else could perceive, and then convincing the world to see things the same way. And for an increasingly international company, it was about transcending a single fixed address. So the agency reports its own history on its website[4].

Maybe that's why the postman had such a hard time delivering the company mail. But after a while, he found the gangway onto the *Klamath*. Eventually, everyone did. Famous visitors included: Marshall McLuhan, Herb Caen, Tom Wolfe, and the Rolling Stones.

As a man who loved to surround himself with performers, artists, and business tycoons, Walter had found his ideal stage perched at Pier 5, on the edge of the continent. For visiting dignitaries, business people, and stars, a trip to San Francisco wasn't complete without an invitation to the *Klamath*.

Parties aboard the ferry were legendary, and so was the branding work that came cascading out of its studios: Levi's, Shell, Quaker Oats, Côte d'Or, Coca-Cola, and British Airways.

One reason Landor was so successful at creating many of the world's top experience brands was because "we were now one ourselves", says the company script on its website.

"Having literally cast ourselves off from increasingly conventional thinking in the industry, we were a living example of the core ideas we preached — differentiation and relevance, risk and results. The legend of the boat preceded us to every pitch, and helped transform us from a national consultancy into an international one synonymous with innovation. It enabled us to more easily attract the best clients and the best talent to serve them".

The *Klamath* became an icon of creativity, not just for those who worked there, but for those who wanted to, who read about the company, and who travelled far to visit the place.

Mr Lim was pleased to be among those and ultimately very pleased with the work of Landor for the airline. These days, Landor's client list of airlines is extensive: Aeroflot, Austrian Airlines, BMI, Cathay Pacific Airways, Garuda Indonesia, Japan Airlines (JAL), Jet Airways, KLM, Malaysia Airlines, S7 (Siberia Airlines) and, of course, Singapore Airlines.

The Singapore office of Landor was run for a while by Thane Madrid, who Mr Lim and his colleagues worked with when refinements were needed or when the livery had to be adapted for the latest aircraft type to appear.

As a leading design company, Landor provided insider access to the varied markets and cultures of Southeast Asia and it is ever ready to talk about its heritage in Singapore — you cannot do better than start at the top with SIA.

It still offers strategic guidance and award-winning design to help clients grow their businesses in some of the fastest-growing economies in the world. Other Singapore-based clients of the firm include: OCBC Bank, Cerebos, SBS Transit, SilkAir, Singapore Exchange, Singapore Post, and SingTel.

Mr Lim would have found an article written by Victoria Corsi of Landor in 2011 very perceptive and interesting as it links the branding of the airline, with its total look and its advertising, and of course, its personalised image in the form of the Singapore Girl[5].

She was asked by *The Hub*, the marketing magazine, to evaluate what she thought of the new or reinvented advertising campaign. It shows the familiar Singapore Girl walking around various iconic locations of the world (Paris, Wuzhen, San Francisco, and Jaisalmer) with a serene look on her face, helping people as she goes.

After gathering opinions both in-house (from her team in Landor's Singapore office) and from others in the creative industry in Asia, she determined that this was "a very polarising campaign":

> *The campaign ticks all the brand-building boxes and enforces its unique iconography without showing a single A380 or SilverKris (until the end frame).*
>
> *Brands need to appreciate that Asian women live in the fastest-growing consumer market in the world. The distribution of wealth in Asian countries is also like no other region: On one end of the spectrum China, Japan, and India's GDP puts them in the top five richest countries in the world. On the other side we have*

Afghanistan, which due to extreme poverty and civil unrest, has the world's second highest infant mortality rate at 150/1,000 live births. This great discrepancy in wealth influences Asian women's purchasing choices, whichever end of the spectrum they live in.

Make sure brands help Asian women become more successful and more beautiful, gain credibility and status, and build a healthy family. Oh, and don't forget: Brands must make her happy, too.

She draws attention, in her article, to the Singaporean fashion label Raoul, created by power couple Douglas and Odile Benjamin which began life in 2002 as a men's shirt company. Later the duo added a successful women's line, and opened 30 stores across Southeast Asia and the Middle East. Raoul debuted in Europe during Paris Fashion Week in 2009.

Another Singapore-based fashion label, Alldressedup has been recognised internationally and is now sold alongside Marc Jacobs and Stella McCartney at online powerhouse net-a-porter.com. With 30 years' experience in luxury fashion and lifestyle retail, founder Tina Tan-Leo believes her successful label appeals to the "bohemian-spirited traveller in every woman".

Raoul and Alldressedup are proof that local Asian design talent is on the meteoric rise, she concludes.

There is little doubt in the mind of Mr Lim and many others who have tasted and approved of the brand experts' work, that Landor Associates is one of the world's leading strategic brand consulting and design firms. Landor pioneered many of the research, design, and consulting methods that are now standard in the branding industry. Partnering with clients, Landor drives business transformation and performance by creating brands that are more innovative, progressive, and dynamic than those of its competitors.

For the record, Landor has 25 offices in 19 countries. Its current and past clients include some of the world's most powerful brands, including Barclays, the Council on Foreign Relations, Diageo, FedEx, Hilton Hotels, Jet Airways, Microsoft, MillerCoors, Procter & Gamble, Taj Hotels Resorts and Palaces, and Verizon.

The selection of Walter Landor and his team to do the SIA livery was an inspired choice. When Mr Lim looks back on it, it had seemed to be the obvious choice — like the Balmain design for the Singapore Girl uniforms.

Landor has done the livery for many airlines since and been called on to tweak or adapt the SIA look for many different aircraft over the years.

The fact that SIA has been wearing pretty much the same outfit on the outside and the inside of its aircraft for such a long time is testament to the thorough evaluation and good judgement of Lim Chin Beng and his team — and those who have followed.

Just like the word "livery" — with its origins that go back centuries to the French and Middle English — the SIA look has stood the test of time. Thanks to a visit by a new airline boss to see a brilliant designer working on a houseboat on San Francisco pier in 1972.

Endnotes

1. The *Klamath* was the very embodiment of everything Walter Landor had built over the last 20 years, and what he hoped to build during the next 20. It would stand as a clear reminder to everyone, inside and outside the company, that branding is a business of passion. That after the customer surveys, design research, and market analysis — rigor he had introduced to the industry — successful branding requires an equal measure of guts, surprise, and delight. For more on the boat and the history of the company Walter Landor founded, see http://landor.com/#!/about/history/the-klamath.

2. From Mr Lim's National Archives interview.

3. In 1977 Walter Landor, founder of Landor Associates, was interviewed by a journalist from KPIX (CBS) for the television show *Evening Magazine*.

4. From the history of the company, recorded in its website, available at http://landor.com/#!/about/history/.

5. Article by Victoria Corsi, which appeared in *The Hub* in 2011, available at http://landor.com/#!/talk/articles-publications/articles/marketing-to-the-modern-asian-woman-trends-to-watch/.

Wheel Music: The young Lim Chin Beng in his preferred mode of travel from his hostel to music lessons and performances — with his double bass in hand — in a trishaw. (A drawing by Australian artist Dave Hickson.)

"If music be the food of love, play on,
Give me excess of it".

(William Shakespeare, *Twelfth Night*)

CHAPTER 5

TALL ON TALENT

This is a "tall story". Singapore Airlines could just as easily have "lost" its first Managing Director to the arts or to sport. The tall young man had a love affair with a musical instrument — the double bass — and he was a keen basketball player.

While he was "distracted" by his University studies and his vocational demands from continuing his musical interests in the professional direction, he also took active interest in sports. If things had gone differently, maybe Lim Chin Beng could have gone to great sporting heights in the basketball world. He was tall — at age 18 he was 6ft 2ins (188cm) and an ideal candidate for a national basketball slot.

But it was not opponents on the court that got in the way, but his determination to study and work that took him off the court. However, he says today that he always enjoyed playing basketball — and has been a keen sports participant and follower. Golf has been more his style in adult years as it has more easily fitted in with his business and diplomatic roles.

He also became more than a spectator for sports and arts. He was ever hopeful that Singapore would someday "produce world class sportsmen/women, musicians, painters, artists, writers, philosophers. Singapore will then be a truly global city pulsating with cultural, social, political and economic vigour".

"On a Little Street in Singapore" — made famous by the Manhattan Transfer — might have been just one of the tunes on the playlist for Lim, the musician, when he performed with a dance band at the Singapore Swimming Club, along with plenty of other popular numbers, when he plucked away on the double bass.

Music was a passion and it could well have been enough to give him a vocation ahead of going into the airline business.

He was one of the very few in Singapore at the time to study music and to take the music exam for O-levels.

Originally he was keen to play the French horn, but the need for a double bass player was more pressing. He kept up music for a good five years while studying. He took lessons from a cellist who was a leader in the orchestra and it was he who invited the young musician to play in the dance band on weekends.

He was also to play his double bass with the Singapore Junior Symphony Orchestra in performances at the Victoria Concert Hall.

Somehow he managed to do his study — the very serious stuff of economics, mathematics and statistics — to balance against his interest in sport and music.

The Raffles Institution — where he was a student 1948–1951 — records an interview with young Lim Chin Beng in its commemorative issue entitled *Inspiring Rafflesians*. The chapter headed "Reach for the Sky", says, among other things, that:

> *When his parents moved to Singapore, he was admitted to Raffles Institution where he excelled at basketball, because of his height. It also enabled him to play the double bass. While he was an undergraduate, playing with a band earned him a monthly income of [S]$200[1].*

Chin Beng recalls the pleasures of playing music — not something he has kept up unfortunately — and the trouble he had to go to, keeping up his practice and his studies. He describes, with a big smile on his face, how he used to travel from his hostel to music lessons with his double bass in tow — protected against the heat and rain — in a trishaw.

He might not have maintained such an active involvement in his music, but he was convinced that young people need to be given the opportunity to excel in the arts as much as they are forced to do well in more academic subjects.

He also made sure SIA and STB gave a high level of support to the arts. And he also made sure he indulged in the arts on his travels — opera in Milan, a concert in Salzberg, a musical or two on the West End or Broadway. His musical tastes were varied. He enjoyed Latin music in Argentina and Spanish guitars in Spain.

He was also instrumental in getting SIA to support the teaching of the arts. He knew of the work of Brother Joseph McNally and his fledgling La Salle College of the Arts. For a while it became LASALLE-SIA College of the Arts and a close working relationship developed between the airline and the school.

It was in 1993 — when Mr Lim was Deputy Chairman of the airline — that SIA management agreed to contribute S$15 million to the construction of new buildings to unite the College's diverse activities under one campus. The College has since reverted to LASALLE College of the Arts, but there is now Singapore Airlines Theatre on the new campus in McNally Street.

Support for the first large scale musicals in Singapore — *Cats* and *Les Misérables* — came from the airline and the tourist board, along with the National Arts Council.

Such was his enthusiasm for fostering creativity and cultural pursuits that he went on record in an interview for the newsletter of the Economics Department of NUS, in the Distinguished Alumnus column, in July 2001:

> *My vision and hope for Singapore is that she attains developed status, and when the basic economic concerns are not so para-mount, that it can strive to become a truly global city excelling not just in economics and technology, but also in the arts, sports, culture, music, etc. When today's youngsters become parents, I hope that they would encourage their children to study what interests them and take part in ECA (Extra Curricular Activities) that they enjoy, rather than learning only to get good examination*

results. Then perhaps we can produce world class sportsmen/ women, musicians, painters, artists, writers, philosophers. Singapore will then be a truly global city pulsating with cultural, social, political and economic vigour[2].

When asked how his study of economics had helped him in his business career he has this to say:

However, while economics provide a strong basic foundation, to be successful you have to build on this foundation and have other interests and skill-sets in addition to what you have from the textbooks. These include an appreciation for the arts, music, sports, foreign cultures, current events worldwide, and in the region, networking skills, social graces and even learning to play golf, which all came in very useful especially when I was Ambassador to Japan. In other words, be strong in your specialisation but also strive to be a "generalist" and broaden your other interests.

On a lighter side, he was delighted to re-tell of his encounters with famous people from the world of the arts and sports.

"I was checking in for a flight — I think from New York to London — when I noticed a man in front of me with a big musical instrument in a case. I was behind him and I heard the check-in person say that you cannot take that instrument into the cabin. The passenger had to tell the girl that he had two tickets — one for himself and one for the instrument. It was a cello and the passenger checking in was none other than the world-famous cellist Yo Yo Ma."

He is pleased to see now the progress Singapore has made both in support of sports and the arts, by providing scholarships, sponsoring major international events and providing some role models — local and imported — for young people to aspire to.

He did his best through the airline and the tourist board to promote major sporting events — tennis and golf featured prominently.

He met plenty of sporting stars when they came through Singapore or took part in events here. He can remember world champion golfer Greg Norman and former tennis number one Bjorn Borg.

He is pleased to witness these days that Singapore is giving the arts and sports — extracurricular activities — the attention they deserve. He is seeing Singaporeans excel by winning medals at international sports events and noticing that artists, writers and musicians are at home performing on the world's stage with distinction.

When he had to select the creative people to "design" the airline — its uniforms, its livery, its advertising, its interiors, its menus — he was forced to look aboard. As he was determined that SIA had a truly international look and feel — there were no designers or artists of note in the early 1970s who were up to the job — he hired Pierre Balmain (French) and Walter Landor (American).

He admits it is different today. Maybe Singapore has the talent to create iconic buildings, fashion items, and products which will make their mark in the world. But the country and the airline still draws on the best it can find. Some will be local and some will be foreign.

He would have to agree now that his hopes have eventuated for Singapore. It has reached the stage when it is "a truly global city pulsating with cultural, social, political and economic vigour".

It is pleasing for this man, a quiet achiever who was tall on talent himself, to see the airline and the country setting high standards for itself and — to use another sporting analogy — "punching well above its weight."

Mr Lim has seen the arts markedly grow in stature at home with global appeal. With events like Arts Stage, the Festival of Arts and Singapore Writers Festival. Where local artists can hold their own with visiting talent and where Singaporeans are actively and creatively participating at overseas festivals.

Music to his ears!

Endnotes

1. From *100 Inspiring Rafflesians, 1823–2003*, by Guan Heng Tan (World Scientific, 2007).

2. From the interview conducted with Mr Lim by Associate Professor Koh Ai Tee on 20 June 2001 published in National University of Singapore's *EconNews* in the "Distinguished Alumnus" column.

Wax Lyrical: The real life model Singapore Girl Lim Suet Kwee (left) with her wax counterpart. (From the Singapore Airlines collection.)

"When the life-size figure of a Singapore Airlines flight attendant is installed this month at Madame Tussaud's waxworks in London alongside such other recently arrived celebrities as Presidents Bill Clinton and Saddam Hussein, it will mark a significant broadening of horizons for one of Britain's most popular tourist attractions".

(Michael Richardson writing in the *New York Times* on 8 June 1993.)

CHAPTER 6

SINGAPORE GIRL

I n the early days of the new airline, Lim Chin Beng recalls he also had the onerous task of selecting candidates for what was rapidly becoming the most glamorous job a girl could have in Singapore.

Whether it was just to wear the fitting, but much-vaunted Pierre Balmain designed outfit, or whether it was the chance to fly to exotic and distant locations. The job of interviewing hundreds of applicants fell to a number of experienced hands, including the Managing Director.

There was a time, Mr Lim recalls with a big smile on his face, when there were sometimes up to two hundred girls a day, lining up for selection as Singapore Girls.

Of course, the airline was wanting girls who "looked the part", but they also had to have good English, be prepared to learn the ropes over three months of intensive training, which included aptitude for first aid, customer service and a certain strength to open and close doors, as well as lift passengers luggage.

Height and weight came into it too, as the airline was determined to maintain the image of the Singapore Girl as befitting the best of international airlines. Mr Lim has repeated many times, that SIA was not going to be seen as just another airline. International standards of inflight service – that other airlines would soon be acknowledging — was SIA's aim.

So, while glamour might have been seen as a big part of it, Mr Lim insisted that those selected for the job had to have many attributes including "personality and character".

It was not just airline management that acknowledged that as part of its efforts to build the image of the Singapore Girl, the airline was running a very rigorous training programme for cabin and flight crew.

Media at home and abroad often reported that the airline's growing repute, and the resulting prestige of the job, has allowed it to be highly selective during its recruitment process, as it receives numerous applications locally and from around the region.

From the beginning, Mr Lim confirms, Singapore Airlines would only recruit Singaporeans and Malaysians as cabin crew, but since 1995, in line with its global expansion, recruitment extended to other countries such as China, India, Indonesia, Japan, Korea and Taiwan to minimise language barriers between cabin crew and travellers.

About 10% of applicants of each recruitment drive are successful and sent for training on their first steps to becoming a Singapore Girl.

For the record, here are some of the strict rules and regulations for the cabin crew, from head to toe, which include[1]:

- The airline requires flight attendants to colour their hair black or dark brown. Flight attendants cannot use highlights.
- Flight attendants with long hair are to coil it into buns or French twists.
- Male flight attendants are to sport short hair above their collar lines and sideburns no longer than the ear lobes. Fringes cannot touch their eyebrows.
- Eyebrows must be shaped, and cannot be fake, be it drawn-on or tattooed.
- Eye shadow must be of the colour prescribed by the company — either blue or brown, depending on skin tone.
- No fanciful, dangling earrings allowed; only studs or pearls.
- Lipstick colour must be among the few shades of bright red prescribed by the company. Pink or plum shades are forbidden.
- No chains and necklaces allowed.
- Only simple bracelets and rings can be worn. Only small and simple watches can be worn.

- A spare *kebaya* must be brought for every flight, including short, one-hour flights.
- Nail polish must be of the bright red colour prescribed by the company. Nails should not be chipped.
- Toenails must be of the bright red colour prescribed by the company. If toenails are unpainted, stockings must be worn as a substitute.
- Safety shoes or covered sandals must be worn during take-off and landing. At other times, flight attendants should wear their batik slippers.

While there might have been some subtle adjustments over the years, Mr Lim insists that the same basic look and class of the Singapore Girl — and boy for that matter — has remained much the same. To stand the test of time is not only a credit to the uniform designer, but all associated with the selection and training of cabin crew, which still maintain the world-leading standards.

An article in CNN's international travel magazine in January 2011 asked the question[2]: Is it time to give the Singapore Girl a makeover?

John Davidson and Charlene Fang for CNNTravel put it this way: "She's cute, friendly and very very smiley, but after 40 years it could be time for Singapore Airlines to modernise its mascot".

Their verdict was that the Singapore Girl is still charming but in desperate need of an update.

They pointed out that Singapore doesn't have many "brands" that stand out in the international community. "There's the Raffles Hotel, the Singapore Sling and its national carrier Singapore Airlines (SIA)". The writers admit that the brand has done more for Singapore than any other. It is clear that SIA in many ways, has been the poster child for Singapore as an efficient, comfortable, safe and welcoming Asian nation.

CNNTravel in 2011 was not the only observers to note that using SIA's stewardesses as the figurehead of its brand was "a masterstroke". Other airlines trade on their technical features and individual services, but SIA built itself on "the grace, hospitality and humility" of its Singapore Girls, the magazine wrote, dressed in the iconic version of the *sarong kebaya* designed by Pierre Balmain in 1968.

It is true that for over 40 years the Singapore Girl has been in every SIA advertisement and publicity effort you can imagine — from TV to newspapers, magazines, direct mail and online. She has been the constant on the SIA journey as the airline went from a tiny Southeast Asian airline to one of the most respected in the world.

But brands, even the strong ones, need to be refreshed, the CNN Travel article points out. So doesn't the Singapore Girl need a modern touch?

For Mr Lim, the Singapore Girl brand — if that is how some journalists see it — is not outdated. It has moved with the times, but it is also consistent and in keeping with the international airline which has modernised in its choice of equipment — aircraft and on board entertainment.

He is quite happy to see the Singapore Girl remain as the powerful symbol of the international airline he helped shape. Which included selecting girls and boys of the right calibre — and look — to represent the airline and to succeed.

He admits that some critics have drawn attention to the Singapore Girl as being sexist and that the cultural references of the old advertisements are outdated. There is some truth to this. It is unlikely that the Singapore Girl of that original adverts would be quite so wide eyed today if she were to hit the streets of London.

Today she is seen as an accomplished woman and a citizen of a first-world country, which was not particularly communicated in its only ads from 1985–1992.

Mr Lim could agree with Richard Johnson, founder and creative head of ad agency The Gang, who says the question of whether SIA should drop Singapore Girl comes up every few years, something he finds strange[3].

"Can Singapore Airlines continue flying high without her?"

Johnson compares it with asking McDonald's to give up Roland McDonald or Disney firing Mickey Mouse. Johnson, who has worked on many different airline advertising campaigns in his career, says "there's a whole heap of reasons to keep the Singapore Girl. She's had years of investment. Why throw away almost 40 years of history? In accounting terms she's an intangible asset".

The Singapore Girl is definitely an aid to recruitment — and still, according to Mr Lim — a mark of excellence, she's more emotional than just a logo, she's award-winning and it's an honest strategy, as the girls used in the ads have all been real members of the airline's staff.

Johnson's view is that SIA has a near perfect combination of brand components.

> *"Rationally we know they are the early adopters of aviation technology, but it's the emotional side to the brand which sways our decision to fly with them."*

For Mr Lim, from the beginning the Singapore Girl has been a "working girl", not some figment of the advertising agency eye. What you see is what you get.

For the CNNTravel writers, they say in the end: "It looks like Singapore Girl is here to stay. She may be middle-aged, a tad behind the times and getting older but she remains relevant. Most importantly she's still putting bums on seats".

"Long may her reign continue", is the final verdict.

And the man who was critical to making decisions in the beginning that gave such a crucial role for the Singapore Girl, Mr Lim couldn't agree more. But he's pleased he does not have to be called on any more to help sort through 200 applicants a day!

Endnotes

1. The "uniform requirements" from Singapore Airlines archives.

2. The CNN article written by John Davidson and Charlene Fang for Travel CNN is available at http://travel.cnn.com/singapore/visit/giving-sia-makeover-488486.

3. Richard Johnson, founder and creative head of ad agency The Gang with his quotes taken from the CNN article.

Mentors All: Singapore's Prime Minister Lee Kuan Yew (seated second from left) was guest of honour at a dinner to celebrate Singapore Airlines' 30th anniversary held at the Neptune Theatre Restaurant in May 1977. On his right is SIA Chairman JY Pillay and on Mr Lee's left is Ngaim Tong Dow, who was Permanent Secretary in the Ministry of Communications at the time, with Lim Chin Beng on the far right.
(Photo from Singapore Press Holdings Library.)

"I never heard that it had been anybody's business to find out what his natural bent was, or where his failings lay, or to adapt any kind of knowledge to him. He had been adapted to the verses and had learnt the art of making them to such perfection."

(Charles Dickens, *Bleak House*)

CHAPTER 7

MEANINGFUL MENTORING

L im Chin Beng had some ideal role models at home and from aboard. As there was no set recipe as to how to be an ideal managing director for a new international airline, he learnt on the job, but he does admit to having some very meaningful and lasting mentors.

He speaks highly of the men he worked for at Malayan Airways, Malaysian Airways and Malaysia-Singapore Airlines. One who stood out was Keith Hamilton who had been seconded from Qantas to Malayan Airways in 1960, the same year the very young trainee Chin Beng joined the airline.

A few years later, the young Singaporean would be assistant to Mr Hamilton when he was Managing Director of MSA. By the time Hamilton left to return to Qantas, Mr Lim had risen to be the longest serving Singaporean in the airline management ranks and made Deputy Managing Director of MSA in January 1971 and already in the role of Managing Director when SIA went out on its own in 1972.

Mr Lim learnt a lot from the Australian and valued the patience and guidance freely given. Mr Hamilton went on to run Qantas, as its CEO in 1980 and it was not long before the two airline heads were literally head-to-head running airlines which competed vigorously against each other for traffic between Australia and Singapore and on the lucrative kangaroo route to Europe[1].

There always remained a deep respect for each other. A value put on the mentoring role he played, and for the great stock Mr Hamilton put on the need for Asian experience to help to get not only MSA but MAS and SIA off the ground.

But his closest "associate" in the early days and later years was none other than Joseph Yubaraj Manuel Pillay, mostly known as JY Pillay to all who worked with him. He could more correctly be recognised as the father of SIA, as he played a parental role, representing the Singapore Government, both as a director of Malaysian Airways and one of the critical directors and co-chairman of MSA during the tumultuous transition and ownership changes in the 1970s.

As he was SIA's first Chairman, while also being a key Government official — he headed the Economic Development (EDB) and Treasury at the time — Lim Chin Beng has a lot to thank Mr Pillay for.

He regarded him as a father figure — even though Mr Lim is two years older than Mr Pillay, who was born in Klang (Malaysia) in 1934 — and as a confidante. And someone who managed the Government relationships, with Malaysia and Singapore, as well as knowing where to go for the source of funding.

Likewise, Chairman Pillay had every confidence in Managing Director Lim. They were a formidable team. The more reserved Lim, even with an economics degree and an in depth understanding of the way an airline operates, was reliant on his chairman for advice and guidance. Pillay was the most senior bureaucrat around and someone who grasped international aviation geo-politics like he was born to it.

Together they were honoured by the international aviation magazine *Aviation Week and Space Technology* as "legends of aerospace for putting SIA on the route to enduring success". That was in 1998 when Mr Pillay was Singapore's High Commissioner to London and Mr Lim was Chairman of the Asian Aerospace and Deputy Chairman of ST Aerospace.

After all these years, JY Pillay and Lim Chin Beng both keep in touch. Both have officially retired from civil service, but not surprisingly Pillay was called back to airline service to help a struggling low cost carrier. He was, until end of July 2014, the Chairman of Tiger Airways Holdings (majority owned by SIA) and remains Chairman of the Council of Presidential Advisers. The latter means that at any time he could be called on to not only advise the

President of Singapore but deputise for him when he is out of the country. That shows how highly regarded he is.

When asked if Mr Pillay had called on him for any advice or help with the budget carrier Tigerair, Mr Lim gives a chuckle and provides no conclusive answer. Remember, Mr Lim himself started a low cost carrier in 2004 and Valuair was sold to JetStar Asia (see chapter 16).

An engineer by training, Mr Pillay was once described by former Prime Minister Lee Kuan Yew as being "equal to the best brains in America".

But his biggest contribution to the economy is seen in his role building Singapore Airlines — Mr Lim at his side — with a staff of 6200 in 1972 in to a world-class carrier. Even in its first year, against all expectations, it recorded a profit around S$15.5 million[2]. Today, SIA has a market capitalisation of US$12.6 billion.

Knowing what was involved getting a low cost carrier started and moving, Mr Lim can understand when Mr Pillay was quoted recently as saying that of all the jobs he has done, the position at Tiger Airways was his most challenging yet. "At Singapore Exchange (SGX), everything ran smoothly. But here, there is always a fire to be fought, opportunities to be sought", he said.

Mr Lim well remembers that Mr Pillay had a rule that any policy paper sent to him should be no longer than two pages.

When asked about this, Mr Pillay was quoted as saying: "The important things are brevity and clarity of thought. Papers should aid administration of management and not be done for elegance".

As if to illustrate the special nature of the "mentoring" relationship between an airline chairman and his managing director, Mr Lim recounts when he was offered as all-expenses paid trip to a conference in Portugal sponsored by a magazine publisher which has been on the receiving end of some of SIA's significant advertising budget. In airline and media parlance it would be described as a "junket", as it would also have allowed plenty of time for golf. Attracted as he was for such a well-deserved and attractive break, Mr Lim mentioned it to his chairman, wondering if he should take up the offer. Mr Pillay, ever mindful of how such "gifts" could be interpreted by others, simply replied, "I wouldn't if I were you".

Needless to say, Mr Lim politely turned down the invitation and has retold the story many times to reinforce the importance of transparency and keeping management "above board".

Talking of mentoring, both would have no hesitation in naming the founding father of Singapore, Lee Kuan Yew himself as a mentor. Whether asked for or not, they would be often on the receiving end of advice from LKY when he was Prime Minister and later appropriately called Mentor Minister.

They also knew from the start that LKY wanted SIA to be a success and endorsed the ambitious plans to make the international airline stand on its own feet. The country's leader put his trust in these two men to make it work — against all odds, it would have seemed. But they were reminded many times — sometimes in the thick of a labour issue, a traffic rights problem or financial strain — that this airline had to make a profit.

Mentors and mentoring goes both ways. There are many hundreds of Singapore Airlines management and staff members, past and present — and many others working for the dozen or so companies where Mr Lim acted as director — who would have no hesitation in naming him for something he did and said that encouraged them. Whether it was when they were selected for overseas jobs or promoted, they knew he had a hand in it. He was patient with staff and he did not hesitate, in his own quiet but very effective way, to pass on his learning and skills to others.

Time and time again, he gave recognition to the work of others, taking little credit himself and certainly wanting to share the limelight. He set an example, he acted — whether acknowledging it or not — as a genuine mentor. He encouraged people with ideas, he fostered enthusiasm and a willingness to work hard.

His door was always open too, and he was ready to counsel those with his timely advice and support.

He demonstrated to all who worked with him and for him that risk-taking was important and necessary at times. He was quoted in the NUS Alumnus column in 2001:

> *You must be willing to take risks if necessary. For instance, after four years in the administrative service, I decided to launch out*

into another career and join the then Malayan Airways even though this entailed a 10% pay reduction. But this temporary 'setback' actually set me on a path to a successful and satisfying career in Singapore Airlines. Nothing ventured, nothing gained.

When asked he would also be quick to encourage staff and all those he encountered "to read widely not only on economics subjects but also on current affairs, technical matters, cultural events etc. The other is not be too short sighted or calculative. For example, you must be prepared to invest time in something you deem important".

Whether mentoring or being mentored, Lim Chin Beng was a willing learner, a caring sharer and a conscientious teacher. He never forced his opinion on others.

He set an example as a cool, calm and collected "conductor" of the business of the airline. He never raised his voice. He was always the gentleman. But as those who worked for him would admit — never underestimate him. He was cool under pressure but he was a tough negotiator. No-one walked over him.

He was not called "Mr SIA" for nothing. He put his stamp on the airline as its first Managing Director and others followed his example.

When he took on the job as Singapore's Ambassador to Japan, no-one gave him lessons in diplomacy. Interestingly, the chapter by Mr Lim in Tommy Koh's book on Singapore's diplomats[3] is headed: "Being an Ambassador the SIA Way".

Described as a "visionary for nurturing and guiding our national flagship to achieve world status", in the book on *100 Inspiring Rafflesians*, the author went on to say that: "A pioneer in the field of civil aviation, he has dared to dream the impossible dream, so that Singapore International Airlines can reach for the sky and fly all over the world — the pride and joy of all Singaporeans".

No mean feat for the man who didn't have a boyhood dream to fly — or run an airline for that matter — but he did have the determination to succeed, to soak up all he could from his mentors, to take risks, to keep an open mind and to bring others with him on a remarkable journey.

To borrow from Charles Dickens words, he had "learnt the art of making them to such perfection". Here's a man who was instrumental in taking the very basic components of an aviation company — like a potter taking the clay — and creating what has become one of the world's leading brands.

He is the first to admit it takes a team to achieve these sorts of results. But a team needs a captain and a coach, just as an orchestra needs a conductor and a leader.

Lim Chin Beng managed — through mentoring and being mentored — to bring out the best in himself and the best in others.

Endnotes

1. Mr Keith Hamilton passed away in Sydney, Australia, at aged 56, while he was Chief Executive of Qantas, according to a report in *The Age* newspaper on 17 December 1984.

2. From a record author by Alvin Chua, available at https://infopedia.nl.sg/articles/SIP_1705_2010-08-10.html.

3. The book mentioned is *The Little Red Dot: Reflections by Singapore's Diplomats (Volume 1)*, edited by Tommy Koh and Li Lin Chang (World Scientific, 2005).

Hands on the Controls: Captain Charlie Chan Soon Kin, the airline's first Director of Flight Operations, who had a distinguished career with SIA and its predecessors. Lim Chin Beng presents him with his long service award. Captain Chan piloted the delivery flight of the first of the airline's new 747s in 1973 to Singapore. (Photo from Singapore Press Holdings Library.)

"The engine is the heart of an airplane, but the pilot is its soul".

(Sir Walter Alexander Raleigh, 1861–1922)

CHAPTER 8

PILOTING PRESSURES

To run an airline is even more demanding than piloting a plane. That became obvious very early on for Lim Chin Beng when it was his job to make sure SIA was ready for take-off.

But he never forgot — having been schooled by experienced men of international airlines — that the men in the hot seat at the front of the jets had to be carefully selected and managed. To clearly demonstrate that it was a truly international airline, he instituted a number of measures to meet the demanding global standards expected.

Pilots, their recruitment and training were key areas of responsibility for senior management of the airline. Of course, the airline inherited some of the pilots already used to flying international routes on long haul aircraft like the Boeing 707 with its predecessor airline, MSA.

And as Mr Lim himself had been put through his paces by past and future bosses of British and Australian airlines (BOAC and Qantas), he knew he had to rely on very good Western-trained and English-speaking pilots. So in the early days of SIA, the most likely voice you would hear giving weather and destination announcements from the cockpit would be Australian or British accented captains with many years' experience. This was always re-assuring to passengers because in the early days, they expected this of an international airline.

Just as he had made sure everything else about the airline — its look, its uniforms, its food and drinks — were of a truly international standard, those men flying the aircraft had to fit the model as well.

With the imminent arrival of the first Boeing 747s, he had to make sure there were the experienced pilots ready to fly them. So a recruitment campaign began and it was not long before SIA had a very well respected cast of pilots not only from Australia and England, but some too with previous flying experience with Air New Zealand, South African Airways, Cathay Pacific, Air India and even an American or two.

But would it not make sense to give Singapore pilots a chance to fly for their own airline? Of course, and a training programme was put in place — again following on from the MSA practice — to put Singaporean and Malaysian pilots, often recruited from the countries' air forces.

One pilot who was well-known to Mr Lim from his Malayan Airways days — one Chan Soon Kin, but also known as "Charlie" — came on board the "new" airline as its first Director of Flight Operations. Captain Chan's appointment showed the importance of having local management, but also putting in to such an important post to the most experienced pilot around.

Some pilots had commercial experience on other aircraft types, but needed additional training to be equipped to fly on the bigger, longer range jets. Initially some of the training was conducted overseas — and still some SIA pilot training is conducted in Australia and other places — but increasingly on the ground simulator training was conducted in Singapore.

Mr Lim recalls making a decision early on for setting up a simulator-based flight training school in Singapore. Of course, it would mean less time spent in the air on more expensive flight training, but the best equipment and the best teachers were required. The recommendation to Mr Lim for the first simulator training set up was big enough to accommodate two or three simulators covering different aircraft types. He said let's go bigger than that — make sure there is room for ten simulators. "We'll need them", he said at the time.

It was the same sort of decision making that showed up when ordering aircraft. After the initial order of two 747s with an option on the third, SIA would more often than not go for an order of ten or more.

To have the youngest and most modern fleet was an early objective for SIA. It would mean big savings in fuel, clearly less operational difficulties or delays, and less time on the ground for maintenance. It made economic sense, but it was also good for the image of the airline. The latest and best equipment meant continually recruiting flight crew members and upgrading its pilots as well.

After Caption Charlie Chan stepped aside, another ex-Malayan Airways pilot took over the controls. The man in charge of flight crew for many years was Maurice de Vaz, who had become chief pilot of SIA in 1979. He was one of the first cadet pilots recruited by Malayan Airways in 1963, the same year he was selected as the best student at the training centre in Scotland where he was training. He became first officer with the airline in 1964 and in 1967 the first local pilot to gain a Singapore flight navigators licence. Appointed captain in 1969, he went on through the aircraft types to become chief pilot for the airline's Boeing 747 fleet in 1979. And went on to be the SIA Director of Flight Operations for many years[1].

The airline's senior management, including Captains Chan and de Vaz, knew only too well how dependent the airline was on its pilots and pilots knew they sometimes had the upper hand. Consequently, many airlines have had a stormy relationship with pilots' unions over the years and had difficulty keeping up with pilot demands.

Things came to a head for SIA as early as 1980 when the Singapore Airlines Pilots' Association (SIAPA) called for a members' work-to-rule action and, in doing so, disrupted the schedules of several flights.

Looking back on it, Mr Lim admits there were "a few problems from some of the pilots, when they decided to go slow".

The problems became serious and *The Straits Times* reported at the time that "Three SIA pilots and a flight engineer, who were sacked after they refused to continue their Dubai to London flight after it landed at its stopover point in Zurich on Nov 16, have been charged with carrying out illegal industrial action"[2].

As if sacking and court action was not enough, they also had to face the wrath of Singapore's no-nonsense Prime Minister Lee Kuan Yee. It was reported at the time that Mr Lee had insisted on a meeting at the Istana with SIAPA executive could members. He personally confronted the pilots and as a consequence, the association was de-registered and the officials of the union prosecuted.

Mr Lim — responsible for running the airline at the time — welcomed the "intervention" of the Prime Minister, who threatened to "close down the airline" if the pilots and their union did not behave.

This was very consistent with the message from Mr Lee at the SIA inaugural dinner, when the country's leader made it plain that that if SIA did not make profits, he would close down the airline.

Pressure on pilots, yes, but also pressure on SIA management to keep the airline flying profitably, while maintaining good labour relations and maintaining its international reputation for reliability and good service.

Maybe a tall order for all, but for SIA senior management they did manage to keep all operations running smoothly and consistently set records as one of the most profitable airlines in the world.

But it was a few years later — when Mr Lim was out of the airline's hot seat and the same Mr Lee was Senior Minister and/or Mentor Minister that things came to a head and SIA pilots were told to toe the line or else.

Nitin Pai, a scholar from the Lee Kuan Yee School of Policy Studies, wrote in his Economy blog on 3 December 2003 that Senior Minister Lee Kuan Yew issued a stern warning to Singapore Airlines pilots on Monday that the Government will not allow them to go slow or work-to-rule, which would damage the airline's reputation and cost it hundreds of millions of dollars in losses in a matter of months. He made the remarks in a speech and a question-and-answer session at the Global Branding Forum. He also spoke about his style of governing compared to that of the younger ministers and the branding of Singapore. We reproduce excerpts from Mr Lee's speech[3]:

> *Right at this moment, we're having a little problem with our pilots.*
>
> *Because of SARS, Singapore Airlines lost a few hundred million dollars that quarter. They persuaded, with the help of the Ministry of Manpower, the unions — not just the pilots' union but the five*

unions across the board in SIA — to take pay cuts, adjust work schedules and generally trim down.

…No one can say how mainline carriers will fare in the next one, two years. Budget carriers are coming into Asia and it's a matter of time before they pose the same challenge to mainline carriers as they do in America and now increasingly in Europe.

…Both management at SIA and the pilots' union, and all the unions in SIA, know that when the Government decides that its industrial relations is a key factor in its progress, in its economic well-being, and it says no, it means no.

History records that relations between the labour unions and the group management has been testy at times, particularly after a series of wage cuts, retrenchments, and early retirement affected staff morale during and after difficult economic conditions such as the SARS outbreak in 2003[4].

The Airline Pilots Association-Singapore (ALPA-S) alone had been involved in no less than 24 disputes with group management since its registration in May 1981. It was formed after its predecessor, the Singapore Airlines Pilots Association had 15 EXCO members charged and convicted for initiating illegal industrial action in 1980 in the wake of disputes with management and the SIAPA was deregistered on 26 February 1981. On 30 November 2003, the Ministry of Manpower (Singapore) amended the Trade Unions Act to overrule an item in ALPA-S's constitution requiring formal ratification from the general membership for negotiation agreements involving the executive committee.

In 2007, the airline was in the spotlight again when ALPA-S disagreed with the management's proposed salary rate for pilots flying the Airbus A380, and the case had to be settled by the Industrial Arbitration Court. The salary ranges of SIA's pilots were made public during the first day of the hearings, and the press noted that the airline's 935 captains who fly the Boeing 777 received higher salaries (over S$270,000) at the midpoint of their salary brackets compared to the company's 36 vice-presidents (S$233,270).

Disputes have also affected the unions, some so severe that they have attracted the intervention of the government. The internal feuding in ALPA-S which led to the ousting of the entire 22-member executive committee on 17 November 2003 was attributed to "internal politics" and theories that it may involve former pilots, including those involved in the deregistration of SIAPA.

On 2 April 2007 the airline group and its unions jointly launched the "Singapore Airlines Group Union-Management Partnership" and the Labour Movement 2011 (LM2011) in a bid to improve their relations, each pledging to be "pro-worker" and "pro-business" respectively. In April 2008, the airline's Chairman Stephen Lee described the relations between management and the unions as "stable and cordial" in the last two years, with better communication between them. He alluded that several government figures, including Minister Mentor Lee Kuan Yew, have intervened to help alleviate differences, and that there has been more regular meetings and exchanges between the two sides[5].

For Mr Lim, he needed no reminder that the airline had to be profitable and labour relations were critical. SIA was an important contributor to the Singapore economy, but as Lee Kuan Yew was to tell airline bosses from day one: "If you don't make a profit, I'm going to close down the airline".

This was made clear during traffic rights negotiations that SIA was not subsidized in any way by its Government as recorded in this United Kingdom essay[6]:

> *A staunch believer in free trade and internally driven growth, Mr. [Lee Kuan] Yew made it clear from the start that the "world does not owe Singapore a living". For example, in the air transportation sector, Mr. Yew's government declared that SIA, although the national carrier, would not receive any subsidies, protection, financial assistance, or economic benefits from the government. It would have to sink or swim based on its own resources and ingenuity. Singapore literally adopted a free skies approach whereby foreign flag carriers from other countries were welcome to serve the city-state without any restrictions. This meant heightened competition for SIA right from the start.*

It certainly helped Mr Lim during his years as Managing Director and Deputy Chairman of the airline that Government — and particularly Mr Lee Kuan Yew himself — took such a close interest in the running of the airline. And the Government put such a strong emphasis on the fact that the airline had to manage for success.

Success and style is what the airline fostered and when asked to describe his style of management, Lim Chin Beng says he did have an open door policy and he was always prepared to listen to all sides when there were decisions to be made. He does say he had heard on the grapevine that some union officers claimed that every time they have a problem, they come to see him. Apparently they said, "I just sit there and nod and smile but they go out of the office happy".

All the signs of a true diplomat and negotiator, industry leader and airline boss *par excellence*!

Endnotes

1. Reference to Captain Maurice de Vaz in *SIA: Take off to Success* by Roy Allen (SIA, Singapore, 1990).

2. Report in *The Straits Times*, on 10 December 1980 headed "Three sacked pilots and engineer charged".

3. This was reported, including considerable extracts from Lee Kuan Yew's speech at the time by Nitin Pa, who is founder and fellow for geopolitics at the Takshashila Institution, an independent networked think tank and editor of *Pragati — The Indian National Interest Review*, a publication on strategic affairs, public policy and governance. He is a graduate of Singapore's Lee Kuan Yew School of Public Policy from where he obtained a Master in Public Administration (MPA) degree. He is an alumnus of Nanyang Technological University, Singapore. The report is available at http://acorn.nationalinterest.in/2003/12/03/lee-kuan-yew-govt-cannot-let-pilots-have-their-way/.

4. A number of accounts of SIA disagreements with its pilots in 2003 and again 2007 are in the public domain, in newspaper reports, online and in Government statements. Some can be viewed at National Archives (of Singapore).

5. The statement by SIA Chairman Stephen Lee has been widely reported and still appears in Wikipedia and other places, including http://www.saciol.com/world/transportation/singapore_airlines.

6. Read more at http://www.ukessays.com/dissertations/business/singapore-airlines-a-strategic-re-look.php#ixzz38edeePqg.

Jumbo Journey: At the Boeing Seattle plant, the first two 747 jumbo jets ordered and manufactured specially for Singapore Airlines, getting ready for their delivery flight across the Pacific to Singapore. (From the Singapore Airlines collection).

"The Wright Brothers created the single greatest cultural force since the invention of writing. The airplane became the first World Wide Web, bringing people, languages, ideas, and values together".

(Bill Gates, the founder of Microsoft)

CHAPTER 9

PLANE MAKERS

Orange Grove Road has a special place in the mind and heart of Lim Chin Beng. A real estate promoters dream, the heavily treed avenue is regarded as one of Singapore's most prestigious residential districts.

One describes it thus: "the area's tranquil, quiet and exclusive suburban atmosphere almost conceals the fact that the bright lights, big city experience of Orchard Road is literally around the corner".

It is also the street where Mr Lim has lived since he came back from Tokyo, a far cry from the airline's home at Changi Airport, with offices built around the edge of the largest column free hangar in the world. Even further in the mind's eye from the massive "homes" of the world largest plane makers, like Boeing's massive Everett and Seattle plants.

But the people of the airline and plane makers themselves did come to this tranquil location to do business. To negotiate and sign deals. For Mr Lim it has extra special memories.

The street's most well-known "residence" is the Shangri-la Hotel. It has also been the location where some important events have taken place.

One of the most important for Mr Lim happened in the Shangri-La ballroom in 1986 when he was awarded the title Businessman of the Year and presented with the "trophy" by the man who was to become Singapore's Prime Minister a few years later in 2004, Lee Hsein Loong, then the Minister of

Trade and Industry and son of the founding Prime Minister of Singapore Lee Kuan Yew.

His achievements in business were recognised many years earlier and when in 1972 as Managing Director of the newly-minted Singapore Airlines, he had to do the honours at a dinner at the same Shangri-La hotel to mark an agreement to spend more money than he would ever had the authority to do before.

The airline sponsored the dinner on 26 July 1972 to mark the occasion. The agreement was with Boeing Commercial Aircraft Company for the purchase of two 747-200 jets for delivery a year later. The cost Mr Lim had to sign off on was S$185.25 million.

It was the airline management's first big purchase decision after negotiating successfully with their Malaysian counterparts to split the MSA airline in two. SIA would inherit the existing longer haul Boeing 707s and some of the shorter haul 737s, as it had also agreed to take over all the major international routes out of Singapore, along with the existing corporate headquarters in Robinson Road and the aircraft facilities at Paya Lebar airport.

Going with Boeing was important for Mr Lim. He had worked with the airline through its transition from Malayan Airways to Malaysia-Singapore Airlines (MSA) and was used to seeing, hearing and flying on Boeing aircraft. To complement the existing 707s and 737s and before the signed for 747s would arrive in 1973, SIA purchased some more 707s to go into service immediately.

It was at the time the first order of 747s from any Southeast Asian airline and SIA was to become one of the biggest and most loyal jumbo jet buyers in the world. It would also be by 1975, one of the biggest and most exclusive Boeing airlines in the world, with seven 747s, fourteen 707s and five 737s.

But Mr Lim tells of his very first and important meeting some months earlier with the key Boeing executive Tex Boullioun who along with representatives of other aircraft manufacturers, was staying at the Shangri-La in 1972[1].

As a negotiating stance, the SIA newbie tells the world's biggest aircraft manufacturer that "we cannot fill the 747. We want to go for the McDonnell Douglas DC10, which is smaller".

In response, Mr Boullioun took out a hotel breakfast menu and on the back
· of it jotted down some figures. Then he told Mr Lim he would make a
proposal. If at the end of each year, SIA's load on the 747 cannot reach up
to the 400 passengers, but it is only up to the DC10, which was 280 passengers, Boeing will compensate SIA for the additional cost of running a
bigger aircraft. But if the airline was to fill the 747 with more than 280, it
would have to share the gain with Boeing.

Needless to say, Mr Lim said no to that deal, which is fortunate, says the grin-
ning Mr Lim many years later. "Otherwise we would be still be paying Boeing
millions now".

However, the two men continued to negotiate on price. In the end SIA did
decide to go with the 747s and made them work, profitably.

But there was much more to the aircraft selection than tense pricing negotiations in Singapore.

Talk to Lim Chin Beng about the trouble the airline management went to
make sure they were buying the best aircraft for the job. Talk to Chai Hon
Yam, the engineer tasked with the detailed, time-consuming job and you
get it chapter and verse.

So much so that Mr Chai wrote a book (yet to be published) about the
evaluation of aircraft based on his work over many years as project manager
for SIA.

His first big job — as requested by Mr Lim — was to see whether the new
airline would purchase Boeing 747s, McDonnell Douglas DC10s or
Lockheed L1011s. A choice of new "wide bodied jets" and it was a process
which other airlines around the world were also going through to suit their
practical needs.

Besides the aircraft itself, also involved in the assessment was the engines
to power these mighty jets. Rolls Royce, General Electric, and Pratt and
Whitney were the three primary engine suppliers and every airline in the
world could have its favourites in the body and the engine department.

Mr Lim had every confidence in his evaluation team, but he had to make
sure the numbers added up, just as Chai had to make sure the engines and
aircraft operated the way they should.

All the things that went into evaluating an aircraft also included looking for the best interior design, the technologies incorporated, the in-flight entertainment systems — which SIA wanted to be only the best — as well as seating materials and seat design, and not just the number of seats that could be fitted in.

So while Boeing got the first orders from SIA and many more since, the airline did cast its eyes often beyond the Seattle plane maker and eventually did select from other aircraft manufacturers for its fleet.

DC10s did come into the fleet in 1978. Altogether nine of the twin-aisled three-engined jets manufactured in Long Beach California were in active service for SIA until 1983. Then the last three DC10s were sold to Biman Bangladesh airlines. The 446th and final DC-10 rolled off production line in December 1988 and was delivered to Nigeria Airways in July 1989. The production run exceeded the 1971 estimate of 438 deliveries needed to break even on the project.

It was not long before McDonnell Douglas was out of the running as an independent plane maker, as it merged with Boeing in 1997. The MD11, which was derived from the DC10 and continued in production until 2001, but only 200 planes in total were built. The MD-11 was assembled at McDonnell Douglas's Douglas Products Division in Long Beach, California (later Boeing's facility).

While Lockheed went out of commercial jet production after its L-1011 tri-jet racked up so few orders compared to the DC-10. The L-1011 was the only passenger jet they ever launched and once they merged with Martin they concentrated on military and transport aircraft. The famous Lockheed Hercules are still seen in the skies all over the world as search and rescue planes and military transporters.

It wasn't long before the European aircraft manufacturer, Airbus, based in Toulouse, France was knocking on the door of SIA. The first Singapore Airlines A300 Superbus went into service in February 1981 and since then SIA has purchased a total of 102 Airbus jets.

Airbus started with smaller aircraft to suit the shorter routes, but then they started to compete with Boeing with aircraft for the medium to long range. And in the end SIA chose the Airbus 380 for the big market — catering for up to 450 passengers and having the range to go non-stop between Singapore and European airports as well as across the Pacific.

And it was the European built Airbus 380 which led to the demise of the original American-made jumbo jet, the 747, at least as far as SIA was concerned. By 2013, SIA had phased out the last of the 747s for passengers, with SIA cargo retaining some for freight purposes only.

Mr Lim made these observations, about plane makers and the aircraft they build for airlines like SIA, when he talked to MBA students from Texas on 4 January 2005:

> *In the immediate future, we will see the introduction of the Airbus A380. This 550-seater aircraft will challenge the Boeing 747 that has ruled the skies for so many years. The travelling public should benefit from lower fares due to the lower seat mile cost of the aircraft. Provided of course, the airlines are not stupid enough to configure the interior of the A380 as shown in the glossy sales brochure, by having massage rooms, a barber and hair dressing saloon, a gym, generous lounge areas etc.*

> *Whilst Airbus will challenge Boeing in the jumbo category, Boeing has not stood still and will, in turn, challenge Airbus in the smaller to midsize aircraft. category. The introduction of the B787 Dreamliner in about four years' time should make Boeing more competitive by having an aircraft that would compete head on with the A340, A330 and the A320 series aircraft.*

> *Both the A380 and B787 developments are important to the air transport industry. Not only are they important in commercial terms, but they are also pioneering the use of new composite materials and design concepts. For the airlines, there will be more choices for aircraft types at more competitive prices, lower operating costs and new passenger in-flight entertainment and internet systems. These will benefit the airlines and the passengers.*

Looking ahead. Doing things for the longer term were always on the mind of Mr Lim when he was in the hot seat at SIA and since.

And he also didn't hesitate to be bold — even take risks — which happened with the first 747 commitments and often since.

What SIA did do repeatedly — as if to shock the airline industry — was "buy in bulk". Normal, perhaps, for some smaller, cheaper consumer products but not normal for aircraft which cost millions of dollars each.

The roll over programme kept the manufacturers happy and SIA got good deals. Not quite two for the price of one — but not unlike that.

Mr Lim knew it gave the airline justification for its claim that it had the youngest fleet in the world. Newer aircraft were definitely more fuel efficient, lighter weight, lower seat mile costs, and greater economies of scale. All an advantage and all went into the economic consideration on top of the engineering assessment of which aircraft to buy from whom. He also points out that most airlines wrote off their aircraft after 15 years. SIA did this after only eight years.

The first really big single order which left mouths gaping was for 20 747-300s in February 1986, worth US$3.3 billion to Boeing. Mr Lim was a member of the management team which approved of that one and many more.

He would also have signed off on the Concorde, if he had the chance. But he did the next best thing. It was another world beater of supersonic proportions. The British-French built Concorde which SIA got its name on but did not have to buy.

It all started when BOAC (now British Airways) wanted to fly the Concorde to Singapore. SIA extracted the concession. If you want to fly the Concorde to Singapore you operate it in conjunction with us.

Mr Lim was pleased as punch when they not only agreed to having one side of the sleek super-jet identified with SIA livery. It was the side where the main doors are, where the passengers go in and out, which is more likely to be seen at airports around the world.

He thinks it was a pity when they had to stop the service with Concorde, mainly because Malaysia would not agree to allow Concorde to continue to operate with the sonic booms impacting it. Even the *New York Times* reported the significance of the occasion on 16 December 1977[2]:

> *The three times weekly supersonic Concorde service between London and Singapore was terminated today because of Malaysia's refusal to permit the use of its territorial air space on "environmental" grounds.*

It was a costly exercise for BOAC — and a pity it had to stop. Mr Lim is a firm believer in the future of supersonic aircraft and expects a return. (See final chapter Flying into the Future.)

While Singapore cannot call itself a "plane making nation", it does have a serious aerospace industry and Mr Lim has played a significant role in the development and management of that business, in addition to wearing his airline hat.

For six years — from 1998 to 2004 — he served on the board and was Chairman of ST Aerospace, the aviation manufacturing and service business of Singapore Technologies Engineering.

The ST Aerospace annual report in 2005[3], records "our deep appreciation to Mr Lim Chin Beng who has stepped down after serving six years as Chairman of ST Aerospace. Through his vision, our Aerospace sector has grown to become an international MRO (Maintenance, repair and operations) brand name and network".

Singapore Technologies Aerospace Ltd (ST Aerospace) had became a leading brand name in the international aircraft industry for maintenance, repair and operations. As an integrated service provider that offers a wide spectrum of maintenance and engineering services through its five capability clusters: Aircraft Maintenance and Modification (AMM), Component Total Support (CTS), Engine Total Support (ETS), Aviation and Training Services (ATS) and Aerospace Engineering and Manufacturing (AEM).

Operating a global network with facilities and affiliates in the Americas, Asia Pacific and Europe, ST Aerospace's customer base included the world's leading airlines, airfreight and military operators.

ST Aerospace also had training arm to provide training services for both pilot and technical vocations. In addition, its air charter entities also have a fleet of helicopter and business jets for a variety of missions, including executive air travel and air ambulance.

He joined the ST Aerospace Board as director on 15 February 1998 and was Chairman of ST Aerospace from 15 April 1998 to 15 July 2004. The Board of Directors of the parent company ST Engineering recommended in March 2005 the appointment of Mr Lim to the main board, as he brings with him "a wealth of experience both in the aviation industry and management". He was earlier co-opted as chairman of the Business Investment and

Divestment Committee of the Company on 9 July 2004 and was appointed independent non-executive director on 31 March 2005.

While he certainly kept his hands in the aviation business in more ways than one for many years — like starting Valuair as a low cost carrier and running the big air shows for Singapore — he was also in demand as a director of companies.

There were so many businesses which had in mind, maybe, that the SIA success story, which was inspired by Lim Chin Beng from the early days, might rub off onto their businesses. If the recipe for growing a successful business in the cut throat world of airlines was in Mr Lim's DNA, maybe they would get some of it too.

So the hospitality industry and the property companies got him on board, as did the media groups and event organisers.

But his negotiating skills with the biggest plane makers in the world were not forgotten. These were put to good use in a diplomatic role and when working on trade agreements for the Singapore Government or winning big contracts for the Changi Airport Group.

Not forgotten were his skills in sussing out the best designers and producers in the world, to make the work of the plane makers come alive inside and out. And to maintain the highest possible standard of international service.

Not only did the biggest aircraft manufacturers in the world want to do business with Mr Lim at SIA but among his biggest admirers — and secret admirers of the airline itself — were others in the business. It was not just the "in-flight service which other airlines talk about", but the way SIA managed to expand its business globally and be one of the most profitable airlines in the world. And win lots of awards too.

The first big plane deal might have been sealed and celebrated at the Shangri-La in Orange Grove Road — close to home — but Lim Chin Beng made sure the airline's horizons were much further afield.

A world away.

Endnotes

1. Ernest "Tex" Boullioun, the renowned former Boeing salesman who was president of the jet maker's commercial-airplane division from 1972 until 1981, went on to set up Boullioun in 1986 as an aircraft leasing company. It was a handshake in 1978 between Boullioun and Frank Borman, president of Eastern Airlines, that led to development of the 757, more can be read at http://seattletimes.com/html/businesstechnology/2002234870_boullioun08.html.

2. An archive of the *New York Times* article is available at http://archive.today/uAbv.

3. The report can be found at http://globaldocuments.morningstar.com/documentlibrary/document/aa36afa40b96a0be.msdoc/original.

Satisfying Service: An image for SIA service captured in an advertisement, created by Ian Batey and his team, featuring the Singapore Girl and drawing attention to "in-flight service even other airlines talk about". (From the Singapore Airlines collection.)

"Service is one of life's great joys. It's a privilege to be in service. It's a great relief, a gift, to be faced with a job that you know absolutely you must do for the benefit of someone else. As long as you give yourself to it. You don't need to worry about anything but doing that job well, and the satisfaction, when you do, is very beautiful".

(Claire Messud, an American novelist and literature and creative writing professor.)

CHAPTER 10

IN-FLIGHT SERVICE

When the newly minted Singapore Airlines got underway as its own branded national carrier in October 1972, it not only inherited MSA's international route network, but it took on a commitment to "in-flight service even other airlines talk about" in more ways than one. International service standards along with the advertising tagline which extolled them.

Starting with connections to over 20 airports across 18 destinations including Europe, the Middle East, Australasia, and parts of South, South-east and North Asia, as its first Managing Director — who had previously been Deputy Managing Director and Managing Director of MSA — Lim Chin Beng had little choice but to go international in every way possible.

International was the favour in the food and drinks, the look and feel of the aircraft inside and out, and — perhaps most important of all — in the in-flight service and its advertising message which boldly claimed "in-flight service that even other airlines talk about".

Mr Lim was determined from the beginning that the airline would "go global"[1]. SIA had a very limited domestic market, so it had to compete worldwide and appeal to the international traveller.

> *So, we consciously say that we had to cater to the taste of the international travellers. So the décor, the aircraft, the food, everything should be for the international travellers but with the Asian courtesy and the Asian touch. That was the formula we adopted.*

Foreign chefs working in Singapore's international-styled hotels were called on to advise on menus. The music and the movies on board had to have international appeal.

SIA also boldly "stepped out of line" when it came to offering economy class passengers a choice of meals, complimentary drinks and free headphone sets, which were normally the preserve of higher-paying business and first class passengers.

Certainly they were seen as innovative offerings at the time and SIA set new service standards for the international airline industry.

Part and parcel of becoming international and excelling in in-flight service offerings, meant — surprisingly perhaps — choosing not be a member of the International Air Transport Association (IATA), which its predecessor MSA had belonged to.

To Mr Lim, IATA was far too restrictive. It even told its member airlines what the seat pitch, or the legroom in the aircraft should be: "An airline wanting to give its passengers greater legroom would be forbidden to do so"[2].

He also pointed out that airfares were strictly laid down by IATA and any airline that dared to give a discount would be fined and, in some countries, even brought to court.

IATA member airline passengers had to "pay for all their hard drinks and their headphones unless of course they were in First Class. But the height of absurdity was when IATA specified the thickness of sandwiches that airlines could serve to passengers".

Besides the Singapore Girl featuring prominently in all its advertising, in-flight service was a key message. The advertising taglines emphasising in-flight service survived for many years. Dreamed up by Ian Batey and his creative team, they stood the test of time.

But Batey admits in his book *Asian Branding: A great way to fly* that SIA was not the first to use such messages[3]:

> *Before Malaysia and Singapore went their separate ways on their national airlines in 1972, there was Malaysia-Singapore Airlines.*

I worked on this advertising account with the Singapore-based management of MSA.

Some key brand identity seeds that subsequently manifested into Singapore Airlines were sown during the MSA period. The service culture was built around the in-flight stewardess. …The slogan "A great way to fly", first appeared in the MSA ads, as did the memorable tagline, "In-flight service other airlines talk about". Many basic ingredients were there, and we were keen to repackage them as part of the Singapore Airlines promise, so long as the brand owner was supportive.

Obviously, the Managing Director of SIA was supportive, as the same Mr Lim had been in senior positions at MSA and had worked with Batey when those slogans were adopted.

Mr Lim does not hesitate to give credit where it's due. He sings the praises of Batey and tells the story of how the English-born Australian advertising man happened to win the SIA account from the beginning.

Ian was working for the advertising company that had MSA as a client. Ian Batey approached SIA management and said he would form his own company to handle the SIA account. Mr Lim says the new airline management had faith in him and said: "Ok, you form your own company, you can have the SIA account."

Mr Lim also recalled when SIA was starting operations to the States, Batey wanted to use the same soft sell approach. "Many of our staff said 'no, no, no American advertisements — short, punchy, right to the point'. Be we took the gamble and we said: 'OK, we use the SIA soft sell'. It was an instant success…"[4]

Setting high service standards and making big claims in its advertising could be a burden for any lesser airline, but SIA used it to its advantage and trained and incentivised its staff to maintain the highest possible levels of service.

Mr Sim Kay Wee, when he was Senior Vice President responsible for Cabin Crew in 2001, added, "Customers adjust their expectations according to the brand image. When you fly on a good brand, like SIA, your expectations are already sky-high. And if SIA gives anything that is just OK, it is just not good enough".

The same Mr Sim, who was to later join Mr Lim in his low cost carrier Valuair enterprise in 2004, also put things succinctly when he said in 2001: "Profit is the applause you receive for serving your customers well"[5].

So the product had to match the message. The experience had to be genuine. And going by SIA's success in winning not only advertising awards but maintaining the "world's best airline tag" for many years, the international in-flight service standards were paying off in more ways than one.

Investing in the most modern aircraft, embarking on aggressive advertising campaigns, dressing its cabin crew in Pierre Balmain-designed outfits and maintaining a truly international appearance, delivered results. Against all expectations that losses would be anticipated in its first year, SIA recorded a very creditable S$15.5 million profit[6].

When a number of senior SIA people were called on to contribute to a study in 2001 and published as "Singapore Airlines: what it takes to sustain service excellence" and put together by Jochen Wirtz and Robert Johnston, they concluded[7]:

> *Every opportunity is taken to develop their staff and systems, deliver great service and re-invent the service by anticipating the potential needs of customers. SIA adopts a holistic approach, creating a "wow" effect by continuously benchmarking against the best in all relevant industries.*
>
> *SIA also strives to maintain consistency in service excellence that at the same time meets the need of every individual customer. This is made possible because of the way they value their staff and customers.*
>
> *SIA management makes it a point to listen to feedback from all quarters and to take appropriate remedial action. The firm belief that training allows for continuous improvement has spurred SIA to invest millions of dollars to train and equip every single staff member to continuously provide excellent service.*

Mr Lim would have to agree that those he helped put in place had their work cut out for them but they managed to maintain those very high standards set at the beginning. In conclusion, the NUS study found two key lessons learned from the SIA story:

> First, service excellence requires a total approach, i.e. excellent customer service is the result of all of the components being in place; the right culture, a clear understanding of the service and a service personality, good people and good systems and processes. The second key lesson is that it does not necessarily need to be expensive. The answer is to improve just a little bit, but all the time and in everything.

Singapore Airlines in-flight service has certainly attracted attention from more than academics and other airlines, and it is not only its own managers who are prepared to give out advice, whether it be good, bad or indifferent. The media has had a field day with SIA over the years.

This glowing tribute came from Dian Hasan, contributor to a US Supplement in the *Jakarta Post* on 22 April 2009. He had this to say[8]:

> Long before branding was even considered a valid approach to estimating a company's strength from a brand perspective, modern-day Singapore Airlines (SIA) was giving the world a taste of its consistent innovation since its founding in 1972, latest technology and aircraft, and above all, a service level that was unheard of in the airline industry, or in SIA's own lingo "an inflight service that even other airlines talk about". And along the way, it collected accolades from the world over as trendsetter, best-in-class and industry leader.
>
> An even more remarkable accomplishment when you take into account Singapore's size — it is one of the world's smallest nations that is not much bigger than the average metro area of any major city. With no domestic market, SIA had to rely on the international market from its inception (it started as Malayan Airways in 1947),

in an industry known to be extremely fickle, prone to rising fuel prices and economic downturns.

In another pleasing affirmation, this time from the Travel and Leisure magazine by Everett Potter in November 2012, confirms that SIA maintained very high in-light service standards over many years[9]:

> *For the 17th year in a row — ever since T+L inaugurated the World's Best Awards — Singapore Airlines has been readers' overall favorite. This year, the airline came out on top in every category: cabin comfort, food, in-flight service, customer service, and value. The 32-inch seat pitch in economy class helps, as do the flight attendants, famous for their above-and-beyond service and sarong and kebaya uniforms.*

In-flight food — never something most of the well-travelled ever have much good to say about — has come in for special media attention, particularly when SIA gets a line-up of international chefs onto it culinary panel[10].

> *Singapore Airlines is so proud of its in-flight food, that they have published an all-star cookbook to celebrate. Nick Harman flew Business Class to Singapore and back in just 48 hours to taste the food and to find out how it's all done.*

Mr Harman notes that Singapore Airlines pioneered the concept of a Culinary Panel to advise on in-flight meals back in 1998 to bring world gourmet cuisine to their passengers and to reflect the cooking of the countries the airline flies to.

The panel meets each year to discuss and focus on new trends and new ideas and to take up the challenges posed by dining at altitude and to bring constant variety to regular travellers.

> *Above and Beyond is the collected recipes of Singapore Airlines International Culinary panel, ten top chefs, including our own Gordon Ramsay, who devise and direct the remarkable food served on Singapore Airlines flights.*

To find these ten chefs in one book is a unique event, the signature dishes of stars such as Georges Blanc, Sanjeev Kapoor, Nancy Oakes, Alfred Portale and Zhu Jun.

Food was not the only ingredient in Singapore Airlines advertising, and as the NUS study showed: "Service excellence requires a total approach, i.e. excellent customer service is the result of all of the components being in place".

Keeping those components has been the job of hundreds of SIA people over the years. Mr Lim might have started it, but.it has been unstoppable ever since, and one of the best examples of airline service excellence in the world.

Ian Batey, as the advertising man who put dreams and reality into words and pictures, summed up how SIA wanted to be seen and known from the beginning[11]:

> *From the very first days of SIA, several things were clear in the mind of the brand owner: the airline was determined to be a highly profitable brand, a worthy global brand, and the best airline brand in the aviation industry. Quite a modest mission, would you not say, for the airline of one of the world's smallest nations!*

But the last words on this subject must go to Mr Lim himself. When asked what his advice would be for young and aspiring officers in the airline industry today, he had this to offer[12]:

> *They must think internationally, not locally. I think too many of our younger people think that what is good for Singaporeans is good enough... You must think really internationally and have a world-class product; not a product that is good enough for Asia. It must be a world-class product if you want to be successful internationally.*
>
> *So you have to think big, you have to be broadminded, you have to have a sense of class — you must appreciate class. What is class? Not something that is cheap... It must be classy. The interiors, the colour scheme, the plates, the glasses. It must be classy, cannot be corny. So, you must have taste.*

For the well-travelled senior airline executive who set SIA on its global course with international service standards, it was vital to have taste and to understand the importance of it by reminding today's youth "to travel internationally to see what it is that other people appreciate".

Endnotes

1. From Mr Lim's National Archives interview.

2. From speech by Lim Chin Beng to MBA Students from the University of Texas, visiting Singapore in January 2005. From Mr Lim's personal archives.

3. From Ian Batey's book *Asian Branding: A great way to fly*

4. From Mr Lim's National Archives interview.

5. From a report published in NUS Business School Research Paper Series, December 2001. Written by Jochen Wirtz and Robert Johnston, *Singapore Airlines: What It Takes To Sustain Service Excellence — A Senior Management Perspective.*

6. On SIA's first profitable year, see http://eresources.nlb.gov.sg/infopedia/articles/SIP_1705_2010-08-10.html?s=Singapore%20Airlines.

7. From Wirtz and Johnston's report, see note no. 5 above.

8. From *Jakarta Post,* dated 22 April 2009, available at http://www.thejakartapost.com/news/2009/04/22/singapore-airlines-powerful-lesson-brand-building.html.

9. From Travel and Leisure (stylised as T+L) article, available at http://www.travelandleisure.com/articles/worlds-best-airlines/2.

10. From Foodepedia.com article, headed "Above and Beyond — Singapore Airlines in-flight meals take taste to new heights". Written by Nick Harman on 22 July 2010, available at http://www.foodepedia.co.uk/articles/2010/jul/singapore_airlines.htm.

11. From Ian Batey's book, *Asian Branding: A great way to fly* (Pearson Ed Asia, 2002).

12. From Mr Lim's National Archives interview.

Tail Spin: As this 1998 photo at Manchester Airport shows, many international airlines line-up alongside Singapore Airlines, but the airline which started the ball rolling to make the UK industrial city accessible to intercontinental carriers had to campaign hard in 1985 to get the right to fly there. (Photo by Aidan O'Rouke, Manchester.)

"First they ignore you,
Then they laugh at you,
Then they fight you,
Then you win".

(Mahatma Gandhi, attributed to the great man and quoted
in *Asian Words of Wisdom*, edited by Steven Howard, Talisman Publishing, 2003.)

CHAPTER 11

INTERNATIONAL RELATIONS

For a diplomat who evolved out of an airline man, international relations was part and parcel of his job. Why was it then, that for a time — in the 1970s and 80s particularly — SIA seemed to be getting into squabbles with practically every other airline in the world?

Over a ten year period, SIA — or more correctly Singapore as a country — had aviation traffic rights disputes with Germany, Australia, New Zealand, Italy, United States, Hong Kong, United Kingdom, Japan and even Sri Lanka.

It must be pointed out that it was the Singapore Government's job to offer traffic rights to other countries and to negotiate rights for its own national carriers. While the media usually show it as a battle between airlines, it should be more correctly seen as country-country negotiation of traffic rights.

Admittedly SIA wanted to move into markets it had no existing traffic rights to but there was a very important principle at stake — freedom of the skies.

During the 80s, mostly while he was Deputy Chairman of the airline, Mr Lim appeared to lead the charge at home and aboard, with near-religious zeal, that for international aviation to flourish there had to be liberalisation in the air and on the ground. He points out that this was the Singapore Government's policy. Singapore welcomed all countries to fly their aircraft to and through Changi Airport.

Time and time again, as SIA was being accused of being "maverick", "upstart" and other even less savoury titles but behind the scenes it was the Civil

Aviation Authority of Singapore (CAAS) personnel in "negotiation mode" to settle disputes and to keep opening up more markets and frequencies for the airline.

Reciprocity was a word not only on Mr Lim's lips when speaking at an international conference, when quietly emphasising the nation's and the airline's philosophy to aviation journalists or across the negotiating table.

Any airline in the world could operate to and through Singapore Changi Airport. That was clearly set out as Singapore's civil aviation policy. Foreign airlines could put down and pick up passengers at Changi and take them anywhere. No restrictions.

In return, all Singapore asked, was that its nominated carrier had the reciprocal rights to do the same. To operate to airports around the world without restriction. Of course, there was no blanket approval. Each country got involved in supporting or opposing traffic rights for "competing" airlines.

Interestingly, the airlines of the two countries who were instrumental in helping to get MSA (the forerunner to SIA and MAS) off the ground — British Airways (previously BOAC) and Qantas — were the very same airlines from nations which openly opposed SIA and Singapore time and time again, frustrating its plans to open up new routes, services or expand its frequencies.

And one of the men Mr Lim would name as one of his valued mentors, he would come up against across the table. Keith Hamilton, who was seconded from Qantas, first to Malayan Airways and later to MSA, went on to be the Chief Executive of the Australian airline.

Mr Lim admits he learnt some of the tricks of the trade from him — including negotiating traffic and landing rights — when he served as Hamilton's assistant, prior to taking on the MD job himself when the airlines split and he took charge of SIA.

This gentleman might have been well trained in the vagaries of running an airline by former and future bosses of big and experienced carriers like Qantas and British Airways (formerly BOAC and Imperial Airways), but was never totally prepared for the cut and thrust, political and diplomatic manoeuvring and the very tough lobbying and bargaining required to win international traffic rights.

Lim Chin Beng learnt the hard way — backed by a chairman who was a financial and political strategist who had received and delivered a few scars — and used all his wiliness and diplomatic skills to keep SIA ahead.

The airline — and the top people leading it — might have been labelled upstarts, mavericks and some names not fit to print, but "protectionism" was the name of the game Singapore kept coming up against.

Like little Oliver in the Charles Dickens classic, Singapore kept asking for more — frequencies, cities/airports, landing rights — and other airlines (and their governments which called them "national" carriers) were not prepared to give anything more to this aggressive Asian airline that wanted to take away their "rightful" passengers.

Let it be emphasised again: landing rights are given away or guarded by Governments. And while the Government of Singapore had a very open door policy and once Changi Airport was operating, a very attractive airport to operate to and through, no-one wanted as many services to the island state as its rapidly growing airline wanted to theirs.

So in the 80s — more than any other time in the airline's short history — brawls were the order of the day. Not that SIA wanted to pick a fight with anyone. Singapore and its airline only wanted to see liberalisation of trade in air services, for the benefit of all.

Lufthansa — now a partner airline in the Star Alliance with Singapore and dozens of other airlines around the world — did not want SIA to fly any more services to Frankfurt or anywhere else in Germany.

Mr Lim has some delight — many years after the events of the 1980s — telling the stories of what Singapore had to put up with or fight against.

They were exciting times. "I loved doing the negotiations for landing rights. That was a real challenge"[1].

Two examples of what happened:

- In Germany, police raided the SIA offices because they said the airline was offering tickets below the approved fares. At the time, the Germans said the fares had to be so much, and no airline could offer less. Mr Lim said he called a press conference and described the police action against

SIA as using tactics that were completely foreign to the airline and more extreme than required. They immediately stopped the action.

- In Amsterdam, the authorities stopped all SIA passengers just before they boarded the aircraft to check tickets and asked passengers how much they had paid. This had the effect of delaying the aircraft. When Mr Lim suggested to the Government that something similar should be done to the Dutch airline in Singapore. KLM passengers were stopped and checked at Changi. This happened with only one flight. "Immediately no more harassment".

With the United Kingdom, Singapore was not getting the traffic rights it wanted, in spite of the fact that British airlines had been flying to and through Singapore for years. The Singapore Government announced it would terminate the agreement with the British, which was taking a big chance because BOAC was obviously contributing to the economy. The permanent secretary at the Ministry of Communications at the time was Ngiam Tong Dow, also the chief negotiator for traffic rights.

But the 12 months' notice to terminate the air services agreement was enough. Soon, there was agreement. Once that was achieved, other European countries followed. Once Singapore got London, then it got Paris. But it was not an easy negotiation, Mr Lim recalls.

The British were very protective of its Heathrow hub and had already had to cruelly deal with its own upstarts like Laker and Virgin. There were battles with other European places, including Italy, while some serious lobbying had to be done in Brussels as well as other European capitals.

Besides Europe, SIA also had to contend with the protectionist policies of Australia, New Zealand, as well as the biggest catch of all, the United States of America.

Generally, there was little difficulty getting the landing rights it needed in Asia, although Japan was sometimes bordering on protectionist, particularly when it observed the growth aspirations of Singapore, compared with its own national carrier JAL, which was not as aggressive as the move progressive ANA, a future Star Alliance partner with SIA.

But the biggest problem within Asia came from, surprisingly perhaps, the only other city state which had the same former colonial master. Hong Kong wanted to protect its Cathay Pacific, which was still — in the 1980s — majority British owned. And until the handover of Hong Kong from British to Chinese, SIA often struggled to get the through landing rights it wanted in Hong Kong. But with the longer range aircraft, Hong Kong could be bypassed but it was both a source of business and a choice destination for Singaporeans and tourists.

With the United States it was a little different as Singapore was prepared to have a very liberal agreement, allowing any number of airlines from America coming into Changi with onward rights, to fly to Australia or Europe. It was a challenge for SIA as it meant it had to compete with more and more airlines. Mr Lim puts it this way: "Because you have to compete, you have to be good. So opening up the skies was really important in making Singapore Airlines a success".

Deregulation of air services started in the United States and eventually spread to the Europe. In the end the US started to sign open skies agreements with a number of countries and Singapore was the first in Asia to have such an agreement with the US.

Lee Kuan Yew had always made it clear that traffic rights were given to foreign countries to benefit the Singapore economy and foster airport growth at Changi Airport ahead of SIA.

When giving a presentation to MBA students from the University of Texas, visiting Singapore in January 2005, a matter of months after he had launched his own low cost carrier, Valuair, he took the opportunity to explain international relations for the airline business[2]:

> *Regrettably, many countries have somehow nurtured a nationalistic attitude towards their airlines which resulted in the countries adopting a highly protectionist aviation policy. The irony is that this has led to the downfall of those airlines because by being overprotected, they become uncompetitive.*
>
> *I often wonder why it is possible for me to buy an American, German or Japanese car, or a Korean TV or Hi-Fi set, or a computer set almost anywhere in the world, but if, for instance, I want to sell an airline seat in another country, it is very, very difficult to*

get the necessary government approval to do so. Why is the airline seat treated differently from the other consumer products?

As you can see, I feel very strongly about this subject of aviation protectionism. This is because I had to weather strong opposition and protectionism from a number of countries in the '70s and '80s when I was involved in the early growth and development of Singapore Airlines. I also had to contend with the "old" IATA, which set ridiculous rules and regulations governing the airline industry.

As many of you in the audience are too young to know or remember what the old IATA regulations were, let me give you some interesting examples: Seat pitch, or the legroom in the aircraft was strictly controlled. An airline wanting to give its passenger greater legroom would be forbidden to do so; airfares are strictly laid down and any airline that dared to give a discount would be fined and in some countries, even brought to court; passengers must pay for all their hard drinks and their headphones unless of course they were in First Class; but the height of absurdity was when IATA specified the thickness of sandwiches that airlines could serve to passengers.

So, when in the '70s, SIA resigned from IATA and decided to give free drinks, free earphones, choice of meals in economy class and more competitive fares, the major airlines saw us as an upstart and called us various names such as pirates, parasites, etc. They saw SIA as coming from a very small country with a population of only about 2 million (at that time) and therefore had no right to carry all that international traffic.

To be fair, I have to say that the IATA of today under the leadership of Mr Giovanni Bisignani, is vastly different from the 'old' IATA. Today, IATA is doing an excellent job in promoting the technical development of the airline industry. It is also very active in security matters, airport improvements, standardisation of procedures and many other functions. In fact, if the membership fees are not too high and we are eligible to join, Valuair will be quite happy to be a member of IATA.

It would a serious omission if an account wasn't given of one of Singapore's success stories during Mr Lim's tenure leading the airline's international relations charge. He remembers addressing the Foreign Correspondents Association in Singapore. SIA was about to go public and offer shares to the staff and general public. He referred to the continual challenges for Singapore regarding traffic rights to other countries, particularly Europe and he referred to SIA's wish to fly to Manchester in the UK in addition to its existing services to Heathrow.

A lobbying campaign was underway in London and the Manchester Airport management was keen to have airlines like SIA fly in with a truly intercontinental service. The mention of Manchester induced a chuckle from some of the British journalists, who hardly saw it as an attractive place. It was seen as a very industrial and boring place, compared to London.

Lim Beng Chin answers coolly and calmly that Singapore and Manchester both saw this as an opportunity to promote tourism, business, trade and cargo between Asia and Europe.

It all started when the management of Manchester Airport in the UK visited Airline House in Singapore. SIA was invited to fly to Manchester.

Never wanting to turn down such an invitation, particularly one that was backed up by a commitment to support Singapore's efforts because it would boost trade and tourism between a well-known industrial centre of Britain with the thriving heart of Asia.

At the time, SIA had daily 747 services to Heathrow and it was certainly not prepared to give up any of those to fly to Manchester. It tested what was thought to be a liberal agreement with London but the application in September 1984 for three services a week to Manchester was rejected.

Not one to give up easily, and with Manchester Airport still keen to host SIA, a major campaign was mounted in the United Kingdom and in Singapore to win the rights to fly to the industrial centre of England.

Members of Parliament and journalists from the United Kingdom were flown to Singapore to learn of the tourism and trade benefits of having an intercontinental airline operating directly between Asia and Manchester.

A case study published in Australia in the book by Jim McNamara sets out how Singapore went about the Manchester campaign and what was communicated to target audiences[3].

It emphasised that:

- There was traffic potential between Manchester and Singapore and that SIA was prepared to develop this;
- Singapore had no objections to other airlines operating Manchester to Singapore;
- SIA operations to Manchester would stimulate development of tourism and trade, and increase employment opportunities in the Manchester area and in the surrounding central and northern regions of the UK;
- Manchester operations would help ease congestion at Heathrow which was becoming a problem;
- Singapore services to Manchester were consistent with the UK Government's policy of encouraging tourism and trade, as well as promoting the interests of consumers and free competition.

In April 1986, after a lengthy campaign of media and lobbying in the UK, the British Government approved Singapore traffic rights to Manchester.

The case study drew attention to the importance of a well-planned and well-executed communications effort in overcoming initial resistance by the British Government, and demonstrated media relations and government relations at work. It helped that the initial invitation came from a British airport as that gave Singapore the allies it needed to promote not only airline services, but the consequent benefits to trade and tourism.

Mr Lim might agree that things have got better for airlines wanting to expand, but the operating environment has got tougher. He observes that his successors still have had to do battle to get some of the services it wants.

He notes that talks first started in 1989 — when he was on the SIA board and in his last year as Chairman of the Singapore Tourism Board — to get beyond rights for SIA to fly from UK across the Atlantic to the US.

Singapore had persisted with its argument that allowing SIA to operate in the UK-US market would promote competition, stimulate demand and benefit consumers through greater choice and better service.

Years of negotiations, improvements made to the Singapore-UK Air Services Agreement and various other liberalisation developments, played their part over two decades in clinching the deal finally in October 2007.

Leong Wee Keat had this to say in the Today newspaper on 12 October 2007[4] that to get the United Kingdom to open up its skies, Singapore negotiators opened up their airline's books. The record said that to dispel the misconception in certain quarters in the UK that Singapore Airlines (SIA) was the beneficiary of State subsidies and preferential treatment from the Government.

According to Singapore's Transport Ministry, the report continued, these quarters felt that granting of transatlantic traffic rights to Singapore's flag carrier could put UK carriers at a disadvantage.

Negotiators pointed to SIA's audited annual reports and stressed that the airline was not a recipient of Government subsidies or special concessions.

Finally, after nearly two decades of negotiations between Singapore and the UK, the signing of a landmark aviation agreement gave the airlines of both countries free access to each other's skies.

For passengers, the Today reporter pointed out, this means being able to take an SIA flight from the UK to third-country destinations, including the United States. "And for SIA, the deal may finally give it a bigger bite of the cherry on the highly-lucrative transatlantic route". Leong concluded by writing that the meeting of minds between the UK and Singapore, according to the Transport Ministry, was the result of "patient negotiations".

Mr Lim could afford to smile on reading that. Some things change and some things never change. "Patient negotiations" were something he had to endure, but he did admit that something dramatic was necessary at times to force the hand of the other party. Singapore could not just sit back and accept police raids on SIA offices or flight delaying tactics as were employed in Europe in his time.

So the quiet achiever, the gentleman and the very diplomatic airline chief had to stand tall and show that to play ball sometimes you had to play rough.

Maybe it was because of his success in fostering international relations — and training his brightest and best in the art of geo-political and aviation industry diplomacy for as long as it achieved the possible — that he was asked a few years later to become Singapore's Ambassador to Japan.

Endnotes

1. From transcript of Interview with Patricia Lee for National Archives Oral History Section in the year 2000, available at www.nas.gov.sg/archivesonline/oral_history_interviews.

2. From speech by Lim Chin Beng to MBA Students from the University of Texas (2005). From Mr Lim's personal archives.

3. The case appeared in *The Asia Pacific Public Relations Handbook*, by Jim McNamara (Archipelago Press, 1992).

4. *Today* newspaper report can be found via the web archives, at http://web.archive.org/web/20080107025949/http://www.todayonline.com/articles/216291.asp.

Well Coached: Lim Chin Beng arriving in style at the Imperial Palace in Tokyo for the first time to present his credentials as Singapore Ambassador to Japan in 1991. (Photo from the Lim family collection.)

"Diplomacy is the art of letting somebody else have your way".

(David Frost, British journalist, 1939–2013)

CHAPTER 12

DIPLOMATIC TO A TEA

For someone in the aviation sector, Lim Chin Beng's choice of words as to how he made the transition into a new type of national service was perfect: "I was parachuted into diplomacy".

So it was not unexpected then when an account of his six years as Singapore's top official to Japan (from 1991 to 1997) was headlined in a book as "Being an ambassador the SIA way"[1].

That Mr Lim enjoyed the experience of being an ambassador for Singapore would be an understatement. Being the perfect gentlemen he is and a most diplomatic person at the best of times, maybe this was his true calling. But it came late in life. Almost an afterthought. And he would not have volunteered for the job — he was invited.

He says it happened this way:

> I was invited to meet with our then Minister for Foreign Affairs, Mr Wong Kan Seng, for a chat. I recall sitting across from him in his office and he asked if I would be willing to become an ambassador for Singapore. The first question in my mind was where would I be posted? When the Minister said "Japan", I immediately agreed. It was probably due to my white hair that I was asked to become an ambassador to Japan! At that time, my impression of Japan was that it was a good place to live.

At the time (in 1991) Mr Lim was still Deputy Chairman of Singapore Airlines. And he did give passing thought at the time he was asked, that he would be once again going on the Government payroll. When he left the Government service in 1960 to join the "risky" airline business and take a 10% pay cut, he did not think that one day — 30 years later — he would become a Government servant once again: this time as a diplomat.

He was able to maintain his SIA directorship but no other outside jobs and was told in no uncertain terms that any of his "other work" — SIA included — would have to be done in his own time. He vividly remembers having to travel at night from Tokyo to Singapore to attend SIA board meetings and fly back the next night.

But he is the first person to admit that his SIA and airline experience was a great asset in doing the ambassadorial job. "My years in SIA helped me to be aware of the importance of etiquette and good manners".

To him, there were two main duties in the life and times of a diplomat. Important as it was to cultivate good relations and keep watching briefs on issues between the two countries, Mr Lim noted that "equal emphasis should also be put on the importance of representing Singapore at many of the formal and social events".

He saw participation at social events, attendance at dinners and receptions as opportunities to show the face of our country and to help make people more aware of Singapore.

"Unfortunately", Mr Lim noted in his observations, "the grading of the officer is based more on their achievements in the former rather than in their efforts in representing Singapore. I remember that I had made it a priority to attend as many of these events as possible".

He also was keen to pass on the lessons learned — typical of an airline man — when his two terms came to an end:

> *I leave three lessons for future diplomats.*
>
> *First, make it a point to attend the less formal events on behalf of the country. It is at these events that you will also get to meet a wider circle of people than the political circuit. Representational duties are as important as political ones.*

*Second, read widely and cultivate a range of interests so that you
can be engaged on many topics. I found that my interests in travel,
music and golf served me well when I was in Japan.*

*Finally, look after the interests of the companies from Singapore
as they too, are viewed as representatives of Singapore.*

And he was able to refer to what he did by way of good example.
Experiencing the culture and places of Japan was very necessary to Mr Lim.

He admits that his understanding of Japan developed when he was negotiating with many Japanese counterparts while at SIA. In those sometimes
difficult negotiations "you get to learn about your opponents very quickly".

So building on that knowledge, when he arrived in Japan, he made every
effort to travel around Japan and meet as many people as possible.

Of the 47 prefectures of Japan, he had visited 40 of them. Sometimes, these
were visits that were part of the tour of ASEAN ambassadors.

"Other times, Winnie [Mrs Lim] and I would go on private trips to some
of these beautiful places. I remember the first time when I was presenting
my credentials to the Emperor of Japan, he had asked me if I had visited
outside of Tokyo. I told him that I had yet to visit the other parts of Japan".

So when he was making his farewell call on the Emperor, "I was pleased
that I could name two of my favourite places outside of Tokyo — Miyajima
Island, near Hiroshima and Jodogahama, north of Miyako in Iwate
Prefecture".

The mention of his wife Winnie in this context also encourages Mr Lim to
tell of what he found to be his most important asset in his time in Japan:
"My wife was my secret weapon. In reality, spouses, particularly the wives,
play a very important role in diplomacy".

He recounts the story of how after a few months into his first term, he
hosted dinner for a few of the senior ambassadors in the diplomatic corps
in Tokyo and also a Vice-Minister of the Japan Foreign Ministry (equivalent
to Singapore's Permanent Secretary).

"The other ambassadors had spent many more years than me in Japan and
had not been successful in inviting the Vice-Minister to their dinner events.

They were very surprised when I, a newly-arrived ambassador, succeeded in doing so".

His wife Winnie had played golf with the Vice-Minister's wife. Through the good offices of his wife, they accepted our invitation.

It led Mr Lim to note that it would be "a big mistake to underestimate the importance of the role of the spouse".

In his years in Japan, he observed that many of the politicians and business leaders often appreciated receiving invitations that included their spouses.

Mr Lim made a special mention of the "Role of the Wife" in his contribution to Tommy Koh's book of diplomatic reminisces:

> *The value of my wife's friendship with the other wives was under-scored on another occasion. The Japanese Crown Prince Naruhito was about to marry Ms. Masako Owada.*
>
> *I visited the Imperial Household office and expressed our Government's wish to offer a gift on this special occasion. I recall the disappointment I felt when I was told that only countries with royalty could offer presents.*
>
> *I thought more about it and counter proposed that we could name one of our orchids after Princess Masako. I consulted with the Singapore Botanical Gardens and they offered three types of Orchids — one pink, one white and one red.*
>
> *I went back to the Imperial Household office and asked them to let Princess Masako select the orchid that she liked. I was then informed that we had to choose the orchid that we wanted to present to the Princess. Winnie knew the Princess' mother, Mrs. Owada very well, so again through her good offices, we were able to arrange for Princess Masako to pick the orchid that she liked.*

Mr Lim made the observation that in Japan, in particular, spouses can play a very supportive and important role for the diplomats. So before leaving his posting he had recommended to the appropriate Ministry that any married Foreign Affairs officers who went on posting to Japan without a spouse should only be given a single allowance!

Besides his observations about the role of the spouse and the role of women in Japan, Mr Lim learned that he was able to also make use of his musical interest. Remember, he was a trained musician, being particularly proficient with a large double bass!

He learned that in Japan, learning to sing karaoke is a must. He recalls that after attending a few dinners hosted by the Japanese for visiting Singapore delegations, he found to his embarrassment that no one from Singapore could sing during the post-dinner karaoke sessions.

> *I decided that I should learn a Japanese song so that I can sing on behalf of Singapore. I consulted my Japanese friend who recommended me a song and went to Akihabara to buy the karaoke tape and lyrics for the song. When I showed the song to my Japanese tutor, she was shocked and said that as an Ambassador, I should not sing the song.*
>
> *The song my friend had chosen was a love song. My tutor felt that as Ambassador, I should speak in the most polite form of Japanese and engage only in the finer aspects of their culture. While I was trained to converse with the Imperial Household, the Japanese I learnt, however, did not help me get the best bargain when I went shopping.*

But for Mr Lim it was certainly not a case of all play and no work during his six and a half years in Tokyo.

For a start, he had to play host to many important visitors and the most frequent from Singapore was Lee Kuan Yew, who was most revered by the Japanese.

He had the opportunity to meet and handle arrangements for Minister Mentor Lee Kuan Yew and Mrs Lee as they visited Japan on a number of occasions in his time as Ambassador. When invited to the meetings that MM Lee was speaking at, Mr Lim recalls it was a real privilege to hear him speak and the Japanese were very keen to learn about geopolitics and activities by other countries, including ASEAN and China, in the Asia Pacific, from him.

Lee Kuan Yew was the only Singaporean at the time to be awarded the Grand Cordon of the Order of the Rising Sun by the Emperor of Japan — he was so honoured in 1967 — certainly the highest civilian order and reserved for very senior heads of state or distinguished leaders from home and aboard.

It was in 2004 — seven years after he completed his distinguished years of service in Tokyo — that Mr Lim was conferred the same Order of the Rising Sun and at the time the only Singaporean since Lee Kuan Yew to be so honoured.

Being a diplomat and one appreciated by his hosts as well as the country he served, is no mean feat, but it seemed to come naturally to this well-travelled man of the world.

He rather casually remarks in his own report card of his time of diplomatic services that "I was fortunate in that my two terms in Japan were relatively peaceful. People may say that an ambassador has a good life but it takes only one unhappy incident to ruin your whole term".

He did, however, see many leadership changes in Japan during my period. When a new Prime Minister was elected and a new Foreign Minister appointed, ambassadors were to pay courtesy calls on the new leaders and review relations between the two countries.

"Thankfully, our relations were stable and, by and large, Japan's policy towards Singapore was generally consistent", Mr Lim notes.

He makes a special point, when recalling his Japanese and his SIA experience, that the friendships that he had made through the years that helped him to conclude "with relative ease" the negotiations for a New-Age Economic Partnership between Japan and Singapore.

> *I remember that the ice was broken when the Japan Vice-Minister from Trade and Industry found out we had visited the same massage parlour in Bangkok! I quickly added that I had visited the parlour with my wife.*

He also points out that another difference between the two negotiating teams was that while the Japanese team was made up of mainly men, half of the Singapore negotiating team comprised women.

It was during 2001 and 2002 that Mr Lim was engaged as the chief negotiator to work through and then conclude Singapore/Japan Free Trade Agreement.

He makes the observation — to help others going on to serve in Japan — that in his experience, "there is more myth than reality about the difficulty of working in Japan".

If you work hard and try to understand them, there is actually not much of a cultural gap. "The Japanese may be a bit more formal in the beginning but once you get to know them better, they are quite friendly".

For his part, he found he fitted in very well. Not only to the role but also the place, as he said when he was first asked to go to Japan, that maybe his white hair helped!

He admitted that in a reception line, he could often be mistaken as Japanese. And as the Japanese always bow to each other, he purposely held out his hand to shake the hand of the guest of honour and others as he stood in line, thereby avoiding the customary bows.

He also found it easy to fit into the way of life, and as he did not "stand out in a crowd", he was able to freely walk around the streets with his wife, visits parks and enjoy nature.

He loved living in Tokyo and nothing could compare to that. Of course, he was pleased to be home in Singapore but he does let on that he was asked when he returned to Singapore from Japan if he would take on another diplomatic posting. He was even asked where he would like to go in the world!

But to him, if it was not Japan, he would prefer to stay on home ground and do the various jobs that were waiting for him.

So this parachuted diplomat landed back in Singapore to be given even more Government and private sector roles in the coming years.

But one voluntary position he gladly accepted had a distinctly Japanese flavour. He was made honorary chairman of the tea ceremony society — Chado Urasenke Tankokai Singapore Association — organised by the Japanese community in Singapore.

He proudly says that it remains the only official role he still fulfils in Singapore or anywhere.

All for the sake of diplomacy.

The love of all things Japanese.

To a tea!

Endnotes

1. This quote and a number of others in this chapter are from Mr Lim's own account of his time in Japan in a contribution headed "Being an Ambassador the SIA way" in the book *The Little Red Dot*, by Tommy Koh and Chang Li Lin (World Scientific, 2005).

Dramatic Action: The hijacked Singapore Airlines SQ 117 in March 1991 at Changi Airport. Lim Chin Beng and the airline Chairman JY Pillay watched this drama unfold from the airport control tower. (Photo from Singapore Press Holdings Library.)

"It was like when you make a move in chess and just as you take your finger off the piece, you see the mistake you've made, and there's this panic because you don't know yet the scale of disaster you've left yourself open to".

(Kazuo Ishiguro, *Never Let Me Go*)

CHAPTER 13

DREADED DISASTERS

A steady hand on the controls managed to give Lim Chin Beng a completely clean record during his time as Managing Director of the airline 1972 to 1982 and even during his deputy chairmanship 1982 to 1996. No aircraft accidents or incidents where lives were lost.

He admits he was lucky. And he is prepared to admit that he always dreaded that a call from the Director of Safety or Flight Operations would herald bad news. He learnt from the beginning never to gloat over a competitor's misfortunes in the air or on the ground. There, but for the grace of God…

The airline industry is united in sympathising with its members when any of them have to deal with a crash or disaster of some type.

Financial disasters haunted many airlines and PanAm, America's pioneering international airline which went out of business in 1991, was plagued by the lot, including the dreadful experience of having its 747 with 259 people on board (passengers and crew) shot down over Scotland in 1988. The question has been asked: Was the Lockerby bombing the death-knell for PanAm[1]?

It is often claimed, most notably in the 1988 movie *Rain Man*, that Qantas has never had an aircraft crash. It is true that the Australian international airline has never had a fatal accident in more than 70 years, even though, for the record, Qantas suffered several losses in its early days before the widespread adoption of the jet engine in civilian aviation. But these days, it is financial troubles which plague the Australian airline and it is asking its Government to come to its aid.

Qantas is, however, still top of the list of ten safest airlines in the world, organised by *AirlineRatings.com* — the world's only safety and product rating website — from the 448 it monitored in 2013[2]. Making up the rest of the top ten, with seven stars for safety and in-flight product, are, in alphabetical order: Air New Zealand, All Nippon Airways, Cathay Pacific Airways, Emirates, Etihad Airways, Eva Air, Royal Jordanian, Singapore Airlines and Virgin Atlantic.

Clearly with excellent financial management from the start, SIA has been one of the consistently most successful and profitable airlines over the last five decades, but disasters of another kind plague the airline industry and SIA and its forerunners was not immune.

He was working for Malaysian Airways when in 1964 their only De Haviland Comet crashed, but fortunately as it happened on landing in Singapore, there were no fatalities.

The most difficult and dangerous incident SIA had during his time was on 26 March 1991, when Flight 117, an Airbus A310-300, was hijacked by Pakistani militants en route from Kuala Lumpur to Singapore. It was stormed by the Singapore Special Operations Force. All of the hijackers were killed in the operation, with no fatalities amongst the passengers and crew.

Mr Lim talked about the hijacking and how he and Chairman Pillay spent many anxious hours in the airport control centre at Changi Airport "riding out" the drama.

He also recalls the close call when on 13 July 1983, a Singapore Airlines SQ 21A was forced to shut down three of its engines while flying through a cloud of volcanic ash created by the eruption of Mount Galunggung, about 180 km south-east of Jakarta, Indonesia.

This was a few days after a British Airways BA 009 on 24 June 1982[3], in the same area, sucked volcanic ash in through the intakes which melted in the combustion chambers and stuck to the inside of the jet engines. Within minutes all four engines failed. The crew, however, handled the grave emergency competently and were able to glide far enough to exit the ash cloud. As the engine cooled during descent the molten ash solidified and enough probably broke off to allow air to flow smoothly through the engine, permitting a successful restart. Even so, landing the aircraft was a hair-raising experience as the pilots were virtually blindfolded by a blanket of ash which had scoured and obscured their windscreen.

The BA flight crew attracted international headlines and awards — for the way they handled an extremely severe set of circumstances and survived intact with no casualties. While the SIA flight was not in such a severe situation, coming so close to the more terrifying experience of the BA experience was sufficient cause for alarm for Mr Lim and his people on the ground. These incidents alerted the international aviation industry to the severe risk of flying through volcanic clouds, leading to a policy of avoiding ash at all costs.

While he was no longer on the board of SIA in December 1997, he clearly identified with and was ready to provide support in any way he could to his former colleagues, when Silk Air — a fully owned subsidiary of SIA — experienced the devastating loss of its Boeing 737-300 on a flight from Jakarta to Singapore.

On 19 December 1997, Silk Air Flight MI 185, piloted by Captain Tsu Way Ming, plunged into the Musi River in Sumatra during a routine flight, killing all 104 people on board. The crash was investigated by various groups, with different results. The Indonesian National Transportation Safety Committee, who were lead investigators, stated that they were unable to determine the cause, while the US National Transportation Safety Board (NTSB) concluded that the crash resulted from an intentional act by a pilot, most likely the captain.

The jury under the Superior Court in Los Angeles in 2004, which was not allowed to hear or consider the NTSB conclusions, decided that the crash was caused by a prominent issue inherent in other 737 crashes: a defective servo valve inside the Power Control Unit (PCU) which controls the aircraft's rudder, causing a rudder hard-over and a subsequent uncontrollable crash. The manufacturer of the aircraft's rudder controls and the families later reached an out of court settlement[4].

Earlier in the same year — on 21 July 1997 while Mr Lim was still in Tokyo as Ambassador — he learned of a fatal training incident involving a Singapore Airlines Learjet 31 9V-ATD plane, carrying a trainee pilot and instructor travelling from Phuket to Ranong in Thailand, which crashed into high terrain. The instructor misread the Ranong DME (Distance Measuring Equipment) thereby causing the trainee pilot to descend below minimum altitude.

As if this was not enough, the first major disaster involving a Singapore Airlines passenger flight occurred on 31 October 2000 when SQ 006, a Boeing 747-400, crashed at Chiang Kai-shek International Airport (now Taiwan Taoyuan International Airport) in Taiwan killing 87 people aboard and injuring 82 people after the aircraft took off on a closed runway that had no warning indications and hit construction equipment.

This occurred during the heavy rain caused by Typhoon Xangsane. SQ 006 was the first fatal crash of a Singapore Airlines aircraft and the first fatal crash of a Boeing 747-400. The accident aircraft 9V-SPK was painted in a "Tropical" promotional livery at the time of the accident. After the accident, 9V-SPK's sister aircraft, 9V-SPL, the only other aircraft painted with the promotional livery, was immediately removed from service and repainted with standard Singapore Airlines livery[5].

While nothing can really compensate for the loss of life and the harm to an airline which experiences such a fatal accident, SIA was seen by the industry and the media to have handled the whole experience in an exemplary fashion.

Airlines learn from each other — and help each other — both to be prepared for the worst but also handle such devastating events in a professional manner with senior management being seen to be involved and identifying with the victims and their families, offering more than sympathy to those grieving.

Whether it was close to home or further afield, Mr Lim identified with other airlines which went through dreaded disasters, particularly where it involved some of the same aircraft types as SIA was operating. And in the case of a number of DC10 accidents in one year (1979) it impacted SIA in more ways than one, because it was ordered to ground the aircraft type for some time while investigations continued.

So it was while he was in the SIA's MD hot seat, he watched with dread the ordeal of the DC10's with serious fatalities in the United States of America — Chicago, Mexico City — and the Antarctica, involving established airlines: American, Western and Air New Zealand.

While he was convinced the aircraft itself was as safe as any — it was cleared to fly when the FAA grounding was lifted — and it was established that the American Airlines accident was caused in all likelihood by poor maintenance and not any fault inherent in the DC10. But it wasn't long before SIA decided to dispose of its DC10s to become — once again — an all-Boeing fleet[6].

In more recent times — even if totally retired from all Government or airline roles — Mr Lim could not help but note with alarm and sympathy what MAS has gone through with two very serious disasters within the space of four months in 2014. Of course he not only knows the airline well — as it claims the same parentage as SIA and he has worked with many MAS people in the past — but it involved the people of his former home country.

First, the mysterious disappearance of MH370 and the prolonged search which to date (September 2014) uncovered nothing. Then the shooting down of a MH17 over Ukraine airspace.

Two disasters too close to home in more ways than one. And no former or current airline man or woman could fail to identify with, and feel for, all those involved in the airline concerned, those impacted by it and those investigating. As with any aircraft incident or disaster, the airline industry learns from them.

The purpose of the air investigation process is not only to uncover the reasons for the incident or accident — and determine at what point the accident was inevitable — but also learn the lessons from it to pass on to others.

Every airline — sometimes with the help of IATA — conducts emergency exercises. It also prepares for what they hope will never be, but has to have a plan in place for a crisis. These require "crisis communication" plans and exercises which in the themselves need to be effectively managed and communicated.

Of course airlines — and sometime aircraft manufacturers, aviation and airport authorities, air traffic controllers — must take responsibility and in all cases you expect some impact on the carrier and the industry.

For SIA, while they had DC10s and utilised them well for a number of years, eventually the final three were sold to Biman Bangladesh airlines. But there was even an offer from a South American airline, which Mr Lim refuses to name, because it involved such a novel payment plan.

While the airline was ready to dispose of its DC10s — but not for a song or a bunch of bananas!

Yes, he tells the story that the airline was actually offered bananas as payment. No doubt the country the airline belonged to had more bananas to spare than cash and as Singapore — like any country — would always need to import bananas, the offer seemed to make sense. But, of course, Mr Lim was not going to be involved in such a deal as it could possibly reinforce something he has always said about the image and performance of SIA — there's no away he wanted SIA to be seen as a carrier from a banana republic. Or selling aircraft to a banana republic!

On a more serious note, Mr Lim, has pointed out to students and others, that while there have been tremendous advances and successes in the world of aviation, it has not been without turbulence.

He told the MBA students in 2005 that "in the last few decades, we have seen many booms and busts in the industry and many well-known names have disappeared. But the industry is a resilient one and I am sure that it will continue to grow in the future although perhaps in various different forms. Airlines are restructuring, forming alliances, trimming their fat, and generally becoming more competitive"[7].

He drew attention to the start of the new millennia:

- In 2002 the industry was hit by the terrorist attacks commonly referred to as the 9/11 incident.
- Then in 2003, SARS hit the industry. In those two years alone, the airlines lost US$25 billion.
- In 2004, the industry was hit hard by the huge rise in fuel prices. By the end of the year, the total loss would have ballooned to US$35 billion.

But Mr Lim did see some signs of a recovery appearing.

> *Positive growth is expected this year (2005) and IATA projects a 6% growth in traffic per year from 2004 to 2008, with the Asia-Pacific leading all regions. Cumulatively, the forecast is for a growth of 140% in the Asia-Pacific region between 2000 and 2007.*

> *While the picture may appear rosy, there are still dark clouds in the horizon. Terrorist attacks, mysterious bird flu, the return of SARS, continuing unrest in many parts of the world and increases in fuel prices are some of the factors that are affecting the growth potential of the commercial aviation industry. And of course the recent tsunami disaster was a tragedy. These are all factors beyond our control.*

But to put flying and aviation into context, it is not as dangerous or as unsafe as one might think. Airline crashes are big events and occupy a lot of media attention. But flying is undoubtedly one of the safest forms of transport on earth — or in the air.

Mark Johanson in an article in January 2013[8] for the *International Business Times* noted that in 2012 there was roughly one fatal airliner crash for every 2.5 million flights.

2012 was the safest year for air travel since the dawn of the jet age in 1945, according to recently released data from the Aviation Safety Network (ASN), an independent organisation based in the Netherlands, with just 23 airliner accidents, resulting in 475 fatalities and 36 ground deaths.

Johnson reported that these figures are well below the 10-year average of 34 accidents and 773 fatalities but came as no surprise to Aviation Safety Network president, Harro Ranter.

"Since 1997, the average number of airliner accidents has shown a steady and persistent decline, probably for a great deal thanks to the continuing safety-driven efforts by international aviation organizations such as International Civil Aviation Organization (ICAO), International Air Transport Association (IATA), Flight Safety Foundation and the aviation industry".

Authorities noted that 2012 also marked the longest period in modern aviation history where there was no fatal accident at 68 days. Of the 23 accidents that did occur, just 11 involved passenger flights and most were in two regions: Russia and Africa.

A BBC report, *What is the safest mode of travel?* in 27 January 2012[9] made the point that it's often said that driving in a car is more dangerous than flying in a plane, yet when an aeroplane crashes or a ship sinks, the nonstop media coverage that follows makes that claim hard to believe.

The report quoted from the National Safety Council (NSC) statistics from the US that an average person's odds of dying in an airplane crash in their lifetime is about one in 5000, while the odds of dying in a car accident was about one in 83.

> *While the number of global vehicle passengers and drivers may not be known, the World Health Organization estimates that 1.2 million people die each year in road traffic accidents (roughly half of which are pedestrians, cyclists and motorcyclists).*

Mr Lim would have to concur that road transport — even for a pedestrian — is more dangerous than being up in the air.

That does not give airlines an excuse, but more a determination to keep the skies safe. Every disaster is one that is not only dreaded, but nine times out of ten, is one that shouldn't have happened.

The airline industry invests heavily in training, safety measures and preparing for the worst, but always hoping that with strong management and attention to detail — the SIA way — as well as a bit of luck, every airline can minimise the chance of accidents and incidents. And remain disaster free.

Endnotes

1. See *The Pan Am: Building and the Shattering of the Modernist Dream*, by Meredith L. Clausen (MIT Press, 2004).

2. Article by Geoffrey Thomas, *Qantas the safest airline* (8 January 2014), available at http://www.airlineratings.com/news/201/qantas-the-safest-airline#sthash.X4O8OxCr.dpuf.

3. Read more about the effect of volcanic ash on planes, and for the news report on BA 009, see BBC News (15 April 2010) available at http://news.bbc.co.uk/2/hi/uk_news/magazine/8622099.stm.

4. The Wikipedia entry for this incident is available at http://en.wikipedia.org/wiki/SilkAir_Flight_185.

5. For detailed report on the incident, see http://aviation-safety.net/database/record.php?id=20001031-0.

6. The author has written extensively on the DC10 accidents, most notably the Air New Zealand accident in his book Flight 901 to Erebus (Whitcoulls, 1980).

7. From speech by Lim Chin Beng to MBA Students from the University of Texas, visiting Singapore in January 2005. From Mr Lim's personal archives.

8. Article by Mark Johanson for the *International Business Times* (7 January 2013), available at http://www.ibtimes.com/2012-air-travels-safest-year-1945-997256. See also www.Tata.org/pressroom/pr/Documents/2012-aviation-safety-performance.pdf.

9. The BBC report is available at http://www.bbc.com/travel/blog/20120127-travelwise-what-is-the-safest-mode-of-travel.

Facing the Media: Lim Chin Beng surrounded by reporters during a Valuair launch event in 2004, when he was in the media spotlight, on top of his job as Chairman of Singapore's largest media organisation, Singapore Press Holdings. (Photo from the Lim family collection.)

"I set up Singapore Airlines to make profits. If you don't make a profit, I am going to close down the airline".

(Lee Kuan Yew, Prime Minister of Singapore, at the inaugural dinner of SIA in October 1972.)

CHAPTER 14

MEDIA & MONEY MATTERS

When Lim Chin Beng is quoted as saying "the time I have spent here ranks among the most satisfying and challenging I've ever had in my corporate career" you automatically think he is referring to his airline work place where he spent the best part of his life — 36 years in all — but no, he is actually referring to the four years he devoted to Singapore Press Holdings, most of the time as Chairman of the board.

He was not a media man, in the same way he was not a diplomat. But when he was called on to do more "national service" at the nation's pre-eminent newspaper publisher, he was following in the footsteps of some of Singapore's best-known Government leaders: Lim Kim San, former cabinet minister 1963 to 1981 and S.R. Nathan, who went on to be Singapore's President. And when he passed on the press reigns in 2005, it was to none other than Tony Tan, former cabinet minister, who went on to be Singapore's current elected President.

An illustrious company of men and a company with an important job to do — the largest media company in Singapore involved not only with newspapers, but also magazines, books, radio and television, plus a decent portfolio of property and related businesses.

In his special message to shareholders in the annual report of 2005, he had this to say, recollecting his four years in the media hot seat[1]:

> We had to deal with the 9/11 attacks, SARS, and the merger of our TV and free newspaper operations. Despite our best efforts,

some jobs were lost and this will always weigh on the hearts and minds of the Board.

But we managed to ride the storms, and the Group stayed profitable throughout. For this I must thank our staff — our most valuable asset — who hunkered down and persevered through the trying times.

So Lim Chin Beng had big shoes to fill at SPH and while he saw it as "being asked to do more national service", others saw it as recognition of his exemplary performance at SIA, STPB, as well as through his notable work as Singapore's Ambassador to Japan, where his diplomatic ways, might well be called on in the daily news scramble and the delicate juggling act of freedom of the press and a Government-controlled media.

Would there be room for him to influence policy and practice in the media world? After all, he had been instrumental in creating an international airline which was the envy of the world and did it in a very competitive environment. It had to stand on its own feet with no government subsidies.

Overseeing the management of a media organisation was something Mr Lim had to learn to do, and even armed with his economics degree, he was not trained in the very different media market and environment. But as with his airline management role, he knew he had to make sure the media business remained profitable. He said as much in his special message — "the Group stayed profitable throughout" — which he could say for SPH as he could for his years with SIA.

So money matters were of a primary concern for media as they were for Mr Lim during his airline and tourist board days, as with any of the other businesses he became involved with.

He could never forget the words of Lee Kuan Yew — "I set up Singapore Airlines to make profits" — and just as he knew making profits was a requirement at SPH, along with its important role of building the nation and serving the nation.

He did make the point that before SIA become listed on the Stock Exchange — in 1986 — it was able to operate as a commercial concern and it could think longer term.

He has it on record as saying of his early years at SIA that while being conscious of the bottom line, he could afford to think more of longer term impact, rather than showing half yearly or quarterly results[2].

We could spend money, knowing that the result will come out in a few years' time, not immediately. Airlines are more under pressure now to deliver profits all the time, where we had perhaps the luxury of building the airline for the future.

Even so in its first 18th months or so SIA returned a very healthy profit!

But Mr Lim — whether airline boss or head man of Singapore's pre-eminent media organisation — was not purely a money man. He believed in investing in people and the future. Winning customers and — in the process — winning awards. Making money and making everyone happy.

He was always quick to give credit to others. His SPH message in 2005 referred directly to the staff: "They are among the biggest sources of pride and satisfaction to me at SPH. I must thank our shareholders as well, for their patience and understanding as we sought to maintain the highest returns during the downturns we experienced. It would not have been possible without your help and understanding".

Being in the media might be different to dealing with the media, but Mr Lim's attitude to the press — whether foreign or local — involved respect and openness. Never one to seek media attention, unlike some airline or media bosses — Sir Richard Branson springs to mind — he was measured and helpful, but also cautious and considerate.

In action at a press conference for the airline, he would give carefully-considered answers. Rarely would he extemporise or go beyond giving a straight answer to a question. He even appeared shy on camera or when confronted by insistent questioning.

One on one with journalists, Lim was more comfortable. Journalists were impressed with his knowledge, his experience, his sound business sense and his accessibility.

While he was SIA's Deputy Chairman he would often be on a speaker's platform in different parts of the world and would meet with the media — some very knowledgeable aviation journalists and others with an interest in travel or business.

When he was also Chairman of STPB, he would agree to meet informally with many of the visiting travel journalists when he would quietly and succinctly expound the virtues of Singapore — and its airline.

Mr Lim was not one to be extravagant with the media. He dealt in facts, he dealt with policy, he produced sound economic facts to back up his position and he was convinced — and convincing — when it came to advocating freedom of the skies, for example. He repeated many times to media and on the speakers' rostrum, the necessity of a liberal policy for international aviation. That was all Singapore expected. Reciprocity between countries and their airlines.

He was also someone the media recognised as an international authority on aviation — he had started SIA and made a success of it. He had introduced far reaching and bold plans for the airline. He was someone with his feet on the ground and his eyes to the skies — the future of flying success.

For many years — particularly during his diplomatic days in the 1990s — he was out of the media spotlight. Except for his name appearing in annual reports and an occasional media release, he was not in the media eye.

So out of the blue, it would seem, when he was appointed a director of Singapore Press Holdings and within a year made its chairman, he was in the media once more. This was a high profile position and one occupied by very high profile Singaporeans. Cabinet Ministers and senior civil servants. In the case of two of them, destined to be Presidents of the nation.

Of course, the chairman of the media organisation might well meet and see editors and journalists of his own papers, but he would not see it as his job to influence in any way, what was in the editorial columns or not.

But it was while he was in the top media job that the spotlight was suddenly on him for very different business reasons.

When it was unearthed — by the media in 2003 — that the same Mr Lim was behind the launch of Singapore's first budget airline, to be called Valuair, he became the news! (See chapter 16.)

While media definitely referred to some of his other hats, past and present — including the SPH chairmanship — when stories and reports about the new airline emerged, there was at least one newspaper at the time which had Mr Lim pictured on the front page announcing that SPH was returning S$1 billion to shareholders as "we will have sufficient funds for our growth strategy and in fact, if necessary, an aggressive growth strategy"[3].

On the same page was news that Qantas announced it was setting up a Singapore-based budget airline with Temasek Holdings and two local businessmen as its investors. In the front page story it also mentioned that "Valuair Ltd set up by former SIA Managing Director Lim Chin Beng" was expected to start that year.

Never one to exploit his position for personal advantage, he was at times having to call on all his diplomatic, business and communication skills when the media focus — local and foreign — was not only on his latest airline start-up, but also how SIA was going to compete with a number of budget airlines in Singapore and the region.

One of the primary papers in the SPH stable — *The Straits Times* — even ran a whole page with the dramatic headline: "A Singapore without SIA?" and the introduction by journalist Rebecca Lee[4]:

> *Competition is now at Singapore Airline's doorstep after having snapped at the heels of its full-service rivals around the world. As it welcomes low-cost carriers with open arms, the Government has said that if it has to decide between protecting Changi's air-hub status and losing SIA's standing in the new aviation landscape, it will choose Changi. So how will the low cost carrier phenomenon affect SIA's fortunes?*

Wisely, Mr Lim chose not to be quoted in the article either on SIA's future or that of his new baby Valuair.

But it did serve to remind him — and everyone else — that the national carrier had to stand on its own feet. Just as Lee Kuan Yew had said in 1972 at SIA's commencement: "If you don't make a profit, I am going to close down the airline".

It was a few years later when the International Air Transport Association (IATA) in 2011 gave credit to "Minister Mentor Lee's vision for a liberal air transport policy and a carrier that adhered to free market principles was years ahead of its time"[5].

> They remain critical issues in aviation today. His desire for leadership and change has also endured. SIA was the first airline to offer free headsets and drinks as well as a choice of meals in economy class, the first to fly a Boeing 747–400 commercially across the Pacific, and the first into service with the Airbus A380.
>
> And MM Lee remains on hand to ensure that aviation's contribution to the Singaporean economy — some 220,000 jobs and near 10% of GDP — is never forgotten. In 2004, when the pilot's union voted out its leaders for agreeing a wage deal with management, he was quick to point out that the future of the airline, and of Singapore, should not be jeopardised.
>
> "We have to think about tomorrow, the day after tomorrow, five years down the road, 10 years down the road," he said. "I worried about it before SIA was formed, when it was part of Malaysian Airways in the 1960s, then Malaysia-Singapore Airlines. Every day, I spend part of my time looking at the future."
>
> Singapore Airlines and Changi have become role models for others to follow. Singapore is a small island that looks very big on an aviation map thanks to Minister Mentor Lee's vision.

It was when Lee Kim San — one of LKY's very close Ministerial colleagues — stepped down in 2001 from the board of SPH and when he introduced Lim Chin Beng and others to the board[6].

Lim Kim San announced that four new Directors joined the Board: Mr Lee Ek Tieng, Mr Ngiam Tong Dow and Dr Yeo Ning Hong on 15 March 2001 and Mr Lim Chin Beng on 1 October 2001. He described them as "highly respected and well-tested personalities". He was certain that the Group will benefit from their invaluable experience.

The retiring SPH Chairman said he has indicated to the Board his desire to step down and not to offer for re-election at the forthcoming Annual General Meeting. "The Board has, however, unanimously decided that I should continue as the Executive Chairman and CEO until a new CEO is appointed".

At the same time, Lim Kim San mentioned that the Board appointed Mr Lim Chin Beng as non-executive Chairman designate and will be actively looking for a suitable CEO.

In Lim Chin Beng's time on SPH board which started in 2001, he also made sure the organisation kept to its primary publishing role and in nation building, he also made sure it contributed to the community in other ways, which he believed was its essential corporate social responsibility.

In the 2004 annual report, he said[7]:

> Demonstrating its strong community involvement, SPH contributed to a broad spectrum of programmes ranging from arts and culture, education, conservation, to sports and charity, as well as to the non-profit Press Foundation of Singapore, an Institution of a Public Character set up early last year to promote lifelong learning.
>
> The Company believes that giving back to the society should be part of its corporate culture, and will continue to play a responsible role as a good corporate citizen to enhance the well-being of the community.
>
> Riding on an improving economy, and with a more rational local media market, we look forward to a better year ahead. Barring any adverse development in the geopolitical and economic environment, the Directors expect the Group's operating performance to improve in the current financial year.

Money matters to media organisations as it does to airlines, but Mr Lim has always made sure that the wider community gets to benefit from what he does and from the organisations he leads. Giving credit where it is due and giving back to the community seems to be ingrained in the heart and soul of this man.

We end this chapter with the last words from Mr Lim in his special message of 2005 when he handed over the SPH reigns with these words:

> *The Group will have new leadership with Dr Tony Tan as its new Chairman. Dr Tan's wealth of experience, stature and contacts will be a definite boost to SPH in a fast changing and evolving media industry. All this bodes well for the future of SPH. I know I will retire with the Company in very capable hands.*

Endnotes

1. Singapore Press Holdings 2005 Annual Report. Available at http://sph.com.sg/system/misc/annualreport/2005/SPH_AR_2005.pdf.

2. From Mr Lim's National Archives interview.

3. *Streats* newspaper published by SPH on Wednesday, 7 April 2004. *Streats* newspaper was renamed as TODAY on 1 January 2005.

4. "Low-cost Terminal: Opportunity or threat?" by Rebecca Lee for *The Straits Times* (17 April 2004).

5. Airline International (IATA) article (6 January 2011). Available at http://airlines.iata.org/blog/2011/06/history-forward-thinking.

6. Singapore Press Holdings 2001 Annual Report. Available at http://sph.com.sg/system/misc/annualreport/2001/sph_ar2001.pdf.

7. Singapore Press Holdings 2004 Annual Report. Available at http://sph.com.sg/system/misc/annualreport/2004/sph_ar2004.pdf.

Leading Lights: Lee Hsien Loong, as the then Minister of Trade and Industry, presenting Lim Chin Beng with the Businessman of the Year trophy in 1986. (Photo from the Lim family collection.)

"Good business leaders create a vision, articulate the vision, passionately own the vision, and relentlessly drive it to completion".

(Jack Welch, Chair and CEO of General Electric between 1981 and 2001.)

CHAPTER 15

BUSINESS CLASS

H ere is an airline that has won practically every Business Class award that it can and run a very competitive international business from day one. And here is the man who got it started and made sure it was a well-oiled, well-managed business in every sense from day one.

Besides international awards for the airline as consistently having the best business class, Lim Chin Beng was recognised in a business class of his own at home too.

In 1986, when he was Deputy Chairman of the airline — after he had served as its Managing Director for ten years from 1972 — he was made Singapore's Businessman of the Year.

While the airline was in a class of its own — its Raffles Class envied by many and winner of every possible business class award in the aviation world — it was the man who had brought this airline to life and nurtured it through its first tumultuous ten years, who was being honoured.

And being the humble, modest man that he is, he made sure when he went to receive his business trophy that he was joined on stage by a group of Singapore Girls, along with members of the airlines' operation staff, to share the limelight and credit.

But there was no denying the skill-set of the man they called Mr SIA. Beyond his academic qualifications — BA (Honours) Economics — he had to come up with all the people skills required to run what was rapidly becoming Singapore's biggest business, in terms of staff and revenue.

In those early years — and even now — challenges came from all sides. International relations, competition and constraints, financial pressures, labour relations, marketing and customer service demands.

Yes, competing for staff and competing for business. Making sure Singapore business people were looked as just after as well as the foreign business traveller. Sometime a difficult juggling act as SIA set standards — and provided in flight services that "other airlines talk about" — that were more than an advertising slogan.

Mr Lim was only the second person to receive the Businessman of the Year Award. It was first introduced in 1985 by the daily Business Times in conjunction with DHL to honour the best in the Singapore business scene. In the first year the prize went to Michael Fam, Chairman, of the beverage and property company Fraser & Neave Ltd.

It was no walkover in the businessman stakes. The criteria for the Businessman of the Year Award are categorised into four areas: financial performance, personal qualities, managerial skills, and contribution to Singapore's development[1].

The judges — drawn from the business and Government sector, as well as the newspaper's editors — only considered candidates who have made an outstanding and sustained contribution to his or her organisation.

Further criteria: "In the case of a public company, for instance, he/she must have contributed to an improvement to the returns on shareholders' funds, and sales, in the light of conditions prevailing at the time. Consideration will also be given to the standard of corporate disclosure of the awardee's company".

The judges were also looking for personal qualities, including integrity, entrepreneurial abilities, managerial skills, depth of management, adaptability, tenacity, leadership qualities, productivity, creativity and good labour management.

Tough criteria and few could claim to have met them all as well as Mr Lim did.

The Singapore Business Awards have grown in stature to become Singapore's most prestigious accolades in the business and corporate sectors.

And for the airline which has consistently won awards for all classes, perhaps it is as a business class airline that it has earned most plaudits.

However, there is much more to being a successful airline — or airline boss — than winning awards. SIA had to continually show that it had to make a success in a business sense.

Business people admire business success. It helped when a respected business magazine like *The Economist* in 1991 — when Mr Lim was Deputy Chairman of the airline — wrote this about SIA[2]:

> *It may be the world's 15th biggest carrier, but Singapore Airlines is consistently the most profitable. In the year ending on March 31st 1991, it made a net profit of S$913m ($513m) on sales of S$4.9 billion. Its balance sheets shows a mere S$438m in long-term debt and a cool S$2.1 billion in cash.*

The contrast with American and European airlines, *The Economist* noted, many of which began to haemorrhage cash during the Gulf war and have yet to recover, could hardly be starker. The magazine raised two intriguing questions: how has a tiny city-state with a population of under 3 million, and thus no automatic reservoir of passengers for its national carrier, managed to create a global airline? And can Singapore Airlines maintain its edge?

Of course Mr Lim is not going to take credit for the continued success of the airline in a competitive world of aviation and business, but he was definitely on the same page as his Chairman when Mr Pillay told *The Economist*:

> *Our mission remains inviolable: offer the customer the best service that we are capable of providing; cut our costs to the bone; and generate a surplus to continue the unending process of renewal.*

Run it as a business in every sense. And the business traveller — whether from its home market or overseas — will support you. And Businessman of the Year 1986 couldn't agree more.

Even today — in 2014 — the international *"DesignAir* Top 10" list which rates airlines out of 100, has Singapore Airlines as the only one with an unblemished 100[3]!

"This scoring of 100 from our judges is rare, and well deserved, showcasing how faultless we feel Singapore Airlines' Business Class product is, and securing it first place on our list. Last year we stated that if it is not broken, do not fix it, but Singapore Airlines have done just that". The design magazine pointed out that the new business class seat designed by James Park Associates (JPA) is even better than the previous incarnation of the seat — which is more First Class than business class.

The acclaim continued, "fine china, excellent and extensive menus, beautiful wine pairings and champagne until you are full (and a little giddy) are all reasons to take to the skies with what still is the best airline in the sky". *Design Air* also noted that with a home in Changi airport, the whole experience from booking your flight to arriving at your destination, "is effortless, and is as close as it gets to the jet set yesteryear we all wish we lived in".

But it is not only one rating which gives it tops. Another international survey, reported *by Huffington Post* and the *NewsCom* media in February 2014, has Singapore Airlines as the best of the best for Business Class[4]:

> *We consulted several sources, from SeatGuru.com to London-based Skytrax, which operates the World Airline Awards, a global benchmark of airline excellence based on extensive customer surveys. We also scanned reader surveys from trusted sources like Travel+Leisure magazine and intel from industry insiders like veteran flight attendants and savvy travel bloggers.*
>
> *This much-awarded airline tops the list in many crucial areas, not least its impressive seats, which, according to SeatGuru, are the world's widest, a generous 34 inches on its Airbus A380–800, which flies from Singapore to London and Los Angeles, among other destinations. The cabin also features ample room between each seat, and, thanks to the 1-2-1 layout, gives every passenger direct access to the aisle.*

Hotel Insider's Philippe Kjellgren, quoted in the same article, is a fan as "Singapore's business class is better than first class on most other airlines", he notes. "You get an almost queen-size bed, turndown service and proper linens. If they can do it, why can't everyone else?"

Ask Singapore's 1986 Businessman of the Year how is it that Singapore Airlines has maintained such a good reputation and delivered so much to maintain top spot in Business Class in the world for so long and one gets a typical Mr Lim smile.

He is not prepared to admit that the high standards he set from the beginning — to make SIA a world class airline and not just "a good Asian airline" — has become set in stone. He will say that the inflight service quality that he was responsible for introducing has been maintained even though some airlines — particularly those from the Middle East — are fast catching up.

He will admit that no airline can be complacent and sit on its laurels. And SIA has always made the most effort to keep ahead of the pack when it comes to design, technology, training, and even in the most practical areas like seat width and orientation.

And he will admit that from the beginning SIA set out to appeal to and win over the business traveller.

There is much more to it than clever and creative advertising, the ever present Singapore Girl and having the most modern fleet.

An airline has to deliver. And Mr Lim has made sure — in the same way that he has been acknowledged as one of Singapore's pre-eminent business leaders — that the airline has to work hard to maintain its position in a business class of its own.

Endnotes

1. Criteria and other information on the selection of the Businessman of the Year is found here: http://www.sbawards.com.sg/awards_businessman.html

2. Quote from The Economist (14 December 1991), *Flying beauty: Singapore Airlines.*

3. The *DesignAir* 100 listing in 2014, available at http://thedesignair.net/2013/04/21/meet-thedesignair-judging-panel/.

4. *Best airlines for business class revealed* (13 February 2014), available at http://www.news.com.au/travel/travel-advice/best-airlines-for-business-class-revealed/story-fn6yjmoc-1226825714297

Valued Together: The four who got together as founding directors of Valuair, pictured at Changi Airport where it was the first Singapore budget carrier registered to operate. From left: Jimmy Lau, Natasha Foong, Lim Chin Beng and Arthur Lim. (Photo from the Lim family collection.)

"When something is important enough, you do it even if the odds are not in your favour".

(Elon Reeve Musk, the CEO of SpaceX and Tesla Motors)

CHAPTER 16

VALUE PROPOSITION

L im Chin Beng played the numbers game in 2004. Known to take risks and encourage others to do the same, he was never a gambler. But while he was in his 72nd year, the number 72 became important for him in other ways.

Changi Airport's 72nd airline to take flight turned out to be his latest airline creation, Valuair, with its leased Airbus 320 flying to Bangkok on its first scheduled flight on 5 May 2004.

Singapore's first low cost carrier, Valuair, commenced scheduled operations and the airport management reported at the time[1]:

> With Valuair joining Changi Airport's family of airlines, Changi is served by 72 airlines with more than 3,400 flights to 164 cities in 53 countries.
>
> A send-off ceremony was organized for the 162 passengers on Valuair's inaugural commercial flight. Mr Wong Woon Liong, Director-General of the Civil Aviation Authority of Singapore (CAAS), and Mr Lim Chin Beng, Chairman of Valuair, were on hand to send off the passengers, who were bound for Bangkok.
>
> At Changi Airport, we believe in working closely with our airline partners to achieve a win-win outcome — we will do what we can to create a conducive environment for our airline partners to

make profits, and they in turn help to enhance Changi's status as an aviation hub. We warmly welcome Valuair as the newest member of the Changi Airport community, and look forward to growing a strong partnership with them", said Mr Wong.

Starting an airline was just one of the many things to keep Mr Lim occupied that year and it certainly boosted his media profile. And it wasn't because he was also at the time Chairman of Singapore Press Holdings, the country's premier media organisation and publisher of the dailies, *The Straits Times* and *Business Times*.

He was also Chairman at the time of ST Engineering Aerospace and director of a number of companies. In the same year, he would also be awarded by the Japanese with the highest honour given to a foreigner.

But a question on a few minds in Singapore and elsewhere related to his latest entrepreneurial airline move. And a subhead to the Straits Times article by Karamjit Kaur, Transport correspondent on 2 March 2004 said it succinctly, "Lim Chin Beng tells why he's starting airline at 71". The story continues[2]:

Even some of his friends refuse to let him forget his past, convinced that the "baggage" from his almost 40 years in Singapore Airlines can be a burden.

Mr Lim Chin Beng, however, laughs it off.

The man, who is among the pioneers in the 1960s who built up then-upstart Singapore Airlines to its current world-class status, is today back in the role of building another upstart that is also being called names.

Again, he brushes it off.

Mr Lim is the chairman of Valuair and, yesterday, in an exclusive interview with The Straits Times, the "baggage" tag seems to be a point of contention.

"Not all baggage is bad," he says pointedly, as he declare his aversion to "personality cults".

He admits that running SIA is "more glamorous" but the thrill of starting a new airline is overpowering.

The idea was sparked about three years ago when PSA Corp lost two giant shipping lines to Malaysia's Tanjong Pelepas Port.

It fortified his belief that Singapore needed a budget airline to protect Changi's hub status.

But at 71, does he not want to slow down?

He laughs at the suggestion, saying: "The Singapore Government says that we should not retire since we are short of people who have the experience."

But Mr Lim's foray into a private enterprise effort to launch Singapore's first low cost carrier — with a very different model — hardly endeared him to the current management of the Government-backed SIA he started in 1972. He was even forced to comment very pointedly on the efforts by a number of other airlines including SIA to hit Valuair in this report in the Straits Times on 6 May 2004:

> *The move by Cathay Pacific and Singapore Airlines to slash fares to Hong Kong smacks of bullying tactics, said Valuair chief Lim Chin Beng, adding that the big boys should compete with each other instead.*
>
> *At a pre-launch ceremony to mark Valuair's maiden flight to Bangkok yesterday, he said "they should be watching each other and fighting with each other" rather than putting their efforts into "losing money trying to fight with a budget carrier".*

Tom Balantyne, a long term observer of aviation in the Asia Pacific, reported fully on the rise of low cost carriers and wrote about Valueair's entry in the issue of Orient Aviation magazine which came out on 1 May 2004[3]:

> *A former chairman of SIA, Lim said he started to prepare for the launch of the carrier nearly two years ago after becoming convinced there would be a budget carrier invasion of Asia. "The most important decision was to determine whether the LCC model that*

was so successful in Europe, such as Ryanair, could be replicated in Asia. We came to the conclusion that the answer was no and that you must have something unique".

His reasoning is simple. In a single European market all flights are virtually domestic on one to two hour sectors. In Asia, particularly from a Singapore base, all flights are international and up to four or five hours in duration.

"So the model is different. Because it is domestic in Europe you can afford to compete on the basis of price, not comfort and service levels", said Lim.

"In Asia, our conclusion was that price was not the issue. As long as the price was low enough and there was some comfort and service, you could have a longer turnaround time, seat allocations and interlining. I can say our fare structure will be about 40% below the full service carrier fare. It will be very competitive compared with the average fares of a budget carrier".

Tom Balantyne included in his report that Mr Lim's main partners in the airline included his son, Arthur Lim, who was named director of customer service, but also took on other operational and Government relations roles; Natasha Fong, former vice-president of EDB Investments, and Jimmy Lau, former president of Reed Exhibitions Singapore and ex-managing director of Asian Aerospace. Each held a 12% stake in the venture.

It was Arthur Lim, along with fellow director Natasha Foong, plus two other operational people from Valuair, one from the Civil Aviation Authority of Singapore (CAAS) and two ST Aerospace licensed aircraft engineers, who all flew on the ferry flight of the first A320 departing on 19 March 2004 from Toulouse, France arriving in Singapore on 20 March.

Media attention was something Valuair encouraged and it certainly got more than its share. Attention focussed on the way the cabin crew looked, as well as to the generous seat width. Chua Kong Ho in *Streats* newspaper (29 April 2004):

The cabin crew was, as expected, the centre of attraction during Valuair's media preview flight yesterday.

> *But another feature which quietly stole the show, for me at least, was the legroom of each seat — all 32 inches of it.*
>
> *In Valuair's case, it has three inches more stretching room than other budget airlines.*
>
> *Let's just say I've been on more uncomfortable Y class flights on so-called prestigious "full-service" carriers.*
>
> *So I think the major carriers have a fight on their hands.*
>
> *At least in winning the hearts and wallets of the likes of me — a long suffering member of the cattle class.*

Another journalist saw it differently and did not go for the overtly casual cabin crew style. Sylvia Toh Paik Choo for *The Straits Times* (30 April 2006):

> *For this emerging new bevy of girls, their raring-to-go faces and turbo-charged smiles say the sky's-the-limit!*
>
> *And their outfits, while confirming down-to-earth fares, do tell another story.*
>
> *Valuair's trainers and polo T-shorts scream that they are en route to the community centre for some class — line-dancing, taichi, maybe how to sell insurance also.*
>
> *Okay, it's sporty, and it's casual, and to be sure, great for trundling up and down the aisles dolling out peanuts and the juice.*
>
> *But it's casual-easy when it should be casual-smart. I like profes-sionals at work not to be dressed like me on holiday.*

Valuair showed how transparent and people-oriented it intended to be, by conducting a public survey asking potential customers where it should fly to next. Reported in Straits Times 1 April 2004:

> *Valuair's maiden flight will be to Bangkok. It will also fly to Hong Kong and Jakarta when it starts operating next month.*
>
> *After that the public will decide the carrier's future destinations.*

Singapore's first low cost airline has asked respondents in an online poll to pick from Perth, Phuket, Hanoi, Bangalore, Madras and Xiamen.

But it was back in 2003, many months before that survey was taken, when there was talk in the air about a low cost carrier start-up in Singapore.

Inquiring journalists speculated on who was behind the launch of the planned first low cost carrier in Singapore.

First with news of Mr Lim's involvement was a Channel News Asia report on 20 June 2003 that read: "Former SIA chief executive Lim Chin Beng has been exposed as the mystery man behind plans to possibly set up a budget airline in Singapore".

The next day *The Straits Times* confirmed the story and also stated that "Mr Lim, 70, who is in France for the Paris Air Show, was not available for comment".

The Singapore company registry record showed that Mr Lim was first appointed a director of the company called Valuair (on 12 May 2003), along with three others — Jimmy Lau, Arthur Lim and Natasha Foong.

Some writers pointed out — suggesting that SIA got wind of Mr Lim's involvement and the Valuair registration before the media did — that the established Singapore carrier announced it had its own high level task force "examining the idea of setting up a separate budget carrier".

According to Nicholas Fang, Transport Reporter for *The Straits Times* (13 June 2003) that: "The move (by SIA) comes amid persistent rumours that an unnamed businessmen here is on the verge of announcing a low cost carrier".

And it was on 4 October 2003 that a *Business Times* commentary by George Joseph drew attention to the fact that SIA was aware of the possibility of another airline — outside the SIA-fold — getting in on the Singapore airline market:

When Singapore Airlines chairman Koh Boon Hwee warning SIA management 12 months ago that there was nothing to prevent the

Government from allowing another Singapore airline to operate, there was no doubt in anyone's mind that something was brewing in the airline industry here.

"If someone were to apply for a licence to operate and hub a new airline in Singapore, it would be very difficult for the Government to say no" Mr Koh declared then.

Now, in comes Valuair, a fledging Singapore enterprise, not connected to SIA, which applied for an Air Operators Certificate.

While the writer was correct, but it was an application from a company headed by a man who was not only well connected to SIA in the past (its founding Managing Director and Deputy Chairman), but someone very close to Government, the public and private institutions.

It was announced in *The Straits Times* on 16 April 2004 that Valuair has become the first of four Singapore-based low cost carriers (LCC) to get the nod from the authorities to start commercial services out of Singapore.

The CAAS said in a statement that it had issued Valuair with a Singapore Air Operator Certificate (AOC) yesterday as the LCC had demonstrated the manpower, organisational structure and maintenance capabilities to operate services safely.

Before that there was a flurry of announcements of local partnerships — and partners — for the new airline.

An example of tie up with companies in Singapore, *The Straits Times* reported (14 October 2003), that Valuair had "signed an agreement with DBS Bank to use its 750 ATMs island-wide for ticket payments. The bank and airline also said they were working on an arrangement for DBS to issue credit cards stamped with the airline's name and mark".

Lim Chin Beng said in a statement at the time:

Valuair aims to offer travellers attractive and competitive air fares with the highest reliability of service. Thus it is very important that customers are able to pay for their tickets in an easy and accessible manner.

DBS, with a base of more than four million retail customers, 550,000 credit card holders and over 500,000 Internet banking customers, was a "logical partner", he said.

On 21 October 2003, *Business Times* reported that Valuair will lease two new Airbus A320 aircraft to start up its fleet in March 2004.

The 162 seat aircraft which will have single class layout with leather seats, will be supplied by Singapore based leasing firm Singapore Aircraft Leasing Enterprise (SALE), and delivered from the Airbus production line in Toulouse, France.

While it might have been interpreted as "keeping it in the family", it was no surprise when another announcement was made earlier (3 December 2003), that Singapore Technologies Engineering (STEngg), which gets half of its profits from servicing aircraft, would get the maintenance contract from Valuair when the airline started.

But it wasn't until well into Valuair's 2004 operational mode that it announced who would be its CEO. It was Sim Kay Wee, most recently SIA's Senior Vice-President Cabin Crew. He had planned to retire before being persuaded to join the budget carrier. He had been the airline's public affairs director previously and also spent 17 years overseas working for SIA in cities including London, Japan, Bangkok, Manila and Brunei. This was reported by *The Straits Times* on 6 August 2004[4].

To put things in context and to take a measured overview of the situation, Mr Lim spoke at the PATA annual conference on Jeju Island, South Korea on 19 April 2004 and had this to say about low cost carriers and his plans for Valuair.

Besides providing something of a history lesson on "The world of aviation in its second century", the title of his talk, he couldn't resist speaking about one of his favourite topics — airline deregulation or freedom of the skies. In particular, he noted[5]:

> *One interesting outcome of the US deregulation was the emergence of a number of budget carriers. This was followed by the emergence of budget carriers in Europe. Budget carriers have now come to*

Asia and they will pose a real challenge to the full service carriers. It is interesting to study the mixed reactions of the full service carriers to this challenge.

Some have chosen to ignore the emergence of the budget carriers and are concentrating on carrying the premium passengers. Some are just trimming their costs to be more competitive. And some have decided to join in the fray by setting up their own budget airlines. Whether they really believe that budget airlines are good investments, I am not too sure.

But there is no denying that budget carriers must be credited with kick-starting the travel industry following the 9/11 incident and SARS. Consumers are the biggest beneficiaries in this fight between the budget carriers and the full service carriers. In this scenario, with many factors in play, it is important for governments to have effective competition laws to prevent the dominant incumbents from resorting to predatory pricing.

What are the factors that account for the success of these Low Cost Carriers (LCCs) in the US and Europe?

Firstly, LCCs in the US and Europe operate domestic routes. Their main competitors are the trains, buses and cars. Secondly, they operate on short sectors of one to two hours. Thirdly, they often operate to secondary airports where costs are lower. Service and comfort can therefore be sacrificed. Can we replicate this model in Asia and achieve the same success? I think not.

The environment in Asia is totally different. Therefore when we first started Valuair about one and a half years ago, we decided that Asia needed a different type of LCC. We deliberately made Valuair a unique model, which to my mind is more suited for the Asian market. It is not cost alone but cost plus some service that will attract the Asian travelers.

For an Asian LCC to be able to grow, it must of necessity operate on longer international routes, unless of course you operate in say China or India which have huge domestic markets. Asian LCCs therefore have to compete with Full Service Carriers (FSCs) instead of surface transport.

Eliminating service and comfort altogether on a flight that could last up to four or five hours, will therefore not work. Asian LCCs also have to operate to major airports because secondary airports in Asia are not as well developed as in the US and Europe.

I therefore decided that the model for Valuair would be to firstly, operate to major cities on high density sectors, secondly, operate new aircraft despite their higher lease cost, thirdly, provide greater comfort by having 32 inch seat pitch instead of the usual 29 inches for LCCs, fourthly, provide seat allocation rather than a free-for-all seating arrangement, fifthly, because the sector length could go up to as high as five hours, provide some basic meal service, sixthly, offer a simple and completely transparent fare structure where the passengers will know that what they see is what they get.

In my view, Asian travellers would look at the total product instead of just cost. Of course the basic philosophy of keeping cost low is just as important whether you adopt the traditional LCC model or the Valuair model. Whichever model you adopt, both are still budget carriers and they will be coming to Asia.

For Mr Lim and his growing band of supporters and customers, 2004 was a good start-up year with the airline starting daily flights to Perth Australia on 1 December. It was also consolidating its position as a low cost carrier to be reckoned with for its services to Hong Kong, Jakarta and Bangkok But he knew it was a costly business and becoming a very competitive one.

Whether it was its first entry to Australia that prompted it, or just because the Qantas-owned Jetstar Asia was wanting to grow its business without so many competitors, but six months into 2005 — on 24 July precisely — this news hit the air waves[6].

Singapore-based budget airlines Jetstar Asia and Valuair have announced the formation of a new Singaporean company that will own and operate both airlines.

The new company, which has yet to be named, will be chaired by Geoff Dixon, who is Chairman of Jetstar Asia and CEO of Qantas Airways.

Jetstar's CEO Ken Ryan will be the chief executive of both Valuair and Jetstar Asia.

He will run both airlines.

The airlines are expected to operate in their own right for the foreseeable future with little or no change to the services they offer.

Analysts say both airlines would also be well placed to participate in growth opportunities within the region.

It came as a shock for some, but others in the industry expected it. As has happened with full-service carriers over the years, alliances, mergers and acquisitions were common.

Admittedly, Valuair was the first low-cost airline to begin operations in Singapore, although some do acknowledge it was very different to the others which followed. Even Mr Lim kept referring to a different model.

It was clear that Valuair sought to differentiate itself even before those who would be its competitors got off the ground. Valuair was offering free hot meals, wider legroom and assigned seating, and marketed itself as a low-fare airline.

One report at the time put it down to "rising fuel prices, along with lack of financial backing and the deep pockets of Qantas' Jetstar Asia and Singapore Airlines-backed Tiger Airways" that finally forced the airline to concede defeat in the highly-competitive local scene.

But as Qantas Chief Executive Officer and Jetstar Asia Chairman Geoff Dixon chaired the new company, Lim Chin Beng and his team stepped aside.

Looking back on this critical time for the start-up, Mr Lim says there were limited options for Valuair. Keeping people in their jobs and keeping the Valuair brand flying, made a "sale" to Jetstar Asia look like the best course of action to take.

But as this report and others show, things did not stop for Valuair. Its brand and name was still being carried on flights.

This commentary from the Centre for Aviation sets it out in context some years later (9 May 2013)[7]:

> From 11 September 2005, Valuair began flying twice daily from Singapore to Jakarta. The new daily flight began as VF208 from Singapore to Jakarta, and VF207 from Jakarta to Singapore.
>
> As of 1 February 2008, flights to Jakarta increased to four times daily.
>
> From 23 October 2005, Valuair commenced daily flights from Singapore to Surabaya, VF531 operated from Singapore to Surabaya, and VF532 vice versa.
>
> Flights to Hong Kong were suspended.
>
> From 26 January 2006, Valuair commenced three weekly flights from Singapore to Denpasar Bali. As at 1 February 2008, the service has been upgraded to become four times per week.
>
> Jetstar had the first mover advantage in the Indonesia-Singapore market as a result of its 2005 acquisition of Valuair, which also launched services in 2004. Valuair was able to access the main Singapore-Indonesia routes before any other LCC as it was able to meet Indonesia's "boutique carrier" definition.
>
> Valuair's authority to operate to Indonesia was a main attraction to Jetstar. At the time of the acquisition Valuair served Jakarta as well as Bangkok, Hong Kong and Perth.
>
> Jetstar Asia took over Valuair's non-Indonesian routes while the Valuair operating certificate was retained for the Indonesian market, although over time the Valuair brand and name has been pushed to the sidelines.
>
> Valuair was used by Jetstar soon after the acquisition to launch Singapore-Bali at the beginning of 2006. Valuair subsequently added Singapore-Medan service in 2008 followed by Singapore-Surabaya service in 2009.
>
> Holding onto the Valuair certificate could give Jetstar options down the road should it or its parent Qantas decide to launch a new Singapore-based airline. The AOC could also be sold although that

*would be unlikely given potential buyers of an existing Singaporean
AOC, such as the AirAsia Group, would be competitors.*

To the Valuair team, led by Mr Lim, who put so much time and effort into
getting the airline off the ground, there must be soul searching and self-
questioning: "If only". But life goes on and all the participants are actively
engaged in other businesses and activities.

While Mr Lim clearly says he has "no regrets" in regards to any of his past
experiences, whether in his SIA days, in his many other business involve-
ments, diplomacy, trade negotiations or his foray into the complex, competitive, even cut-throat, world of low cost carriers.

He made a bold move — as he was wont to do — in setting up Valuair. He
showed what was possible and in the process put the "cat among the
pigeons". He started Singapore's first low cost — or more correctly — low
fare carrier, because he wanted to show that Singapore could do it.

He ended up competing not only with established full service airlines, even
SIA, but with new low cost arrivals on the scene, even Tiger Air which had
SIA and Singapore Government backing. Eventually, he decided (with the
support of his team) that there was little viable alternative but to agree to
the merger and eventual sale to Jetstar Asia.

Would he have liked to see things turn out differently? Would he like to
see Valuair today holding its own as a "model" low cost carrier — different
from the rest — but successful and independent?

A smile and a shrug. Ten years after he saw Valuair take off — and 42 years
after he saw Singapore Airlines take to the international skies — he notes
that in mid-2014 there are four low cost carriers certified to operate out of
Singapore, including Valuair in name, along with Jetstar Asia, Scoot and
Tiger Air.

Singapore Airlines is holding its own and its regional subsidiary Silk Air is
still going strong.

He can claim to have started an unstoppable movement in Singapore with
the first of the low cost carriers, albeit with a different model and a different
look.

Competition is good, whether it is from within the country or from outside. And he can only recall — and repeat — something he said many years ago in an interview for a University alumni publication. He said in business you must "be willing to take risks".

"Nothing ventured. Nothing gained".

Endnotes

1. From a press release from Civil Aviation Authority of Singapore (CAAS) is available at http://www.caas.gov.sg/caas/en/About_CAAS/Media/?__locale=en.

2. "Valuair Chief: My Model will work" by Karamjit Kaur (2 March 2004) in *The Straits Times*.

3. "Singapore Shakedown", by Tom Ballantyne (1 May 2004) in *Orient Aviation*.

4. Karamjit Kaur in Straits Times on 6 August 2004.

5. Taken from his speech notes entitled "The World of Aviation in its Second Century" given by Mr Lim at the Pacific Asia Travel Association (PATA) Conference on 19 April 2004.

6. "Jetstar Asia and Valuair form new Singapore company", by Rita Zahara (24 July 2005), *Channel NewsAsia*.

7. "Jetstar Aims to Catch Up in Indonesia After Squandering First Mover Advantage Inherited from Valuair" by Centre for Aviation (CAPA) (9 May 2013). Available at http://centre-foraviation.com/analysis/jetstar-aims-to-catch-up-in-indonesia-after-squandering-first-mover-advantage-inherited-from-valuair-108938.

Airport Shopper: Lim Chin Beng was portrayed as a "shopper of airports" in this framed cartoon which was given to him to mark the completion of six years as Chairman of Changi Airports International. (Photo from the Lim family collection.)

"By the time I left, I had come to realise that the amenities that make an airport exceptional are pretty much antithetical to the beeline nature of airports. And against all odds, Changi is as good at getting you in and out and on your way as it is at welcoming you to stay awhile".

(Karrie Jacobs, contributing editor at *Architect Magazine* and *Travel+Leisure* on why Changi is the best airport in the world.)

CHAPTER 17

AIRPORTS AHEAD

It is perhaps a surprise to hear from Lim Chin Beng that he was reluctant for SIA to move from Paya Lebar airport which had served the airline and its predecessors well for many years.

Changi Airport was ready for its opening in 1981 and of course SIA would be part of it. But it was back in 1977 when the airline discussed the proposed move and as airline boss at the time, he was keen to stay put.

"Yes, I was reluctant to move as we had invested a lot in Paya Lebar and we were at home there. I felt we didn't need to move. But I was over-ruled. On reflection, I admit, I was short-sighted".

He took into account the infrastructure the airline already had at the location that had served as Singapore's international airport from 1955, the main base for Malayan Airways, Malaysian Airways, Malaysia-Singapore Airlines and since 1972, Singapore Airlines. It should also be noted it was the airport for many other international airlines as well.

For a while SIA maintained some of its services — cabin crew training, for example — at Paya Lebar. But its administrative hub and engineering hangar would move to Changi.

Billed as the largest column free hangar in the world at its time and capable of housing three jumbo jets side by side, the massive structure was positioned at the northern end of the runway at Changi and was completed in 1982, the year after the airport opened for passenger services. Wrapped around three sides of the massive structure was the head office for the airline — Airline House.

It was here that Mr Lim made his transition from Managing Director to Deputy Chairman of the airline (in 1982). While he handed over the day to day reins of running the airline to a younger George Chan, he still turned up every day to occupy his Airline House office and continued to involve himself heavily in airline affairs, most notably international traffic rights issues (and opportunities) and managing the sometime delicate relations with Government, airport authorities and other airlines.

It was some years later — in 2007 — when he would be required to once again focus his attention on Changi Airport with renewed interest. He agreed to serve as Chairman of Changi Airports International, the consulting arm of the Changi Airport Group (CAG), which in 2009 had been formed to manage all aspects of the airport management, and separated from the Civil Aviation Authority of Singapore (CAAS) which concentrated on its role as the nation's aviation regulatory authority[1].

For many years, the airport which was regarded as the best in the world was Schiphol in Holland. It wasn't long before Changi surpassed it and became the best in the world. Consistently Changi won international awards, some were organised by travel and aviation magazines, some independently conducted surveys and contests with votes from frequent travellers.

There was one particular award which Changi cherished and it could not help winning it for 25 consecutive years. This was the "Best Airport in the World" title, first conferred on Changi Airport in 1988 and every year since until 2012. The airport's CEO Lee Seow Hiang proudly received the award in September 2012 at a ceremony in London, and said at the time[2]: "This is a great milestone for Changi Airport and we are truly honoured to receive this accolade. In our short history of 31 years, winning this award for 25 consecutive times is strong recognition of the culture of service quality and innovation that has been established in Changi Airport over the years".

These were the same attributes Mr Lim was to emphasise as he led the International division to "sell" its world-leading airport services around the world.

In the past, there were times when airline observers could see SIA and Changi Airport did not always see eye to eye. Maybe when it came to purely commercial reasons, SIA might have considered that CAAS, as the airport managers, were giving better treatment to overseas airlines. But he had to accept that the airport was provided as a facility for all airlines and no special favours could be expected by the national carrier.

Any reluctance by the airline to move its operational base to Changi was soon put aside and airline management concentrated on making a smooth transition while at the same time making sure it maintained its leadership position globally as an airline heading for the top.

But Mr Lim's initial reservation about Changi, was nothing compared to the bigger political decisions that had been made somewhat earlier to invest a lot of money to make Singapore's premier destination for airlines on a large tract of reclaimed land east of the old British air base at Changi.

It was definitely the strong advocacy by Singapore's Prime Minister Lee Kuan Yew that led to the Changi becoming the location of the international-award winning airport, even though some commentators wanted to give due credit also to Howe Yoon Chong.

This report of the current PM's statement applauding the senior Lee's fore-sight must have reinforced his position as the visionary leader and father of modern Singapore.

It is always acknowledged that the Minister of Defence at the time, Mr Howe Yoon Chong, played a pivotal role in the development of Changi Airport. In a speech — in May 2013 — by former minister Lim Boon Heng at the 5th Howe Yoon Chong PSA Scholarship Award Ceremony, he had this to say[3]:

> Back in 1975, Mr Howe had the foresight to push for a new airport to be built at Changi rather than to follow expert opinion to expand the existing airport at Paya Lebar with a second runway. The land at Changi was reclaimed from the sea, an international terminal built from scratch, and the new airport began operations on schedule in July 1981.

Mr Howe's pioneering role in the matter was also honoured in 2012 by the Changi Airport Group, when it launched the CAG-Howe Yoon Chong

(CAG-HYC) Book Prize, a support programme under the Changi Foundation[4].

The Group's press release said:

> As we mark the completion of the upgrading for T1, we fondly remember Mr Howe, a pioneer of Changi, for his spirit of true grit in surmounting difficult and challenging circumstances. Despite the views of experts, Mr Howe determined that Changi Airport was doable within the timeframe set. As it turned out, his assessment proved to be an astute and accurate one.

The last words on this come from Howe Yoon Chong, then Minister of Defence, on the official opening of Changi Airport in 1981:

> Whether we have been extravagant in investing in an airport of this size and level of sophistication is a question worthy of a rhetorical rejoinder. Can Singapore ever afford not to have such an airport?

It must be mentioned that one of key motivations for a move to Changi was prompted by the widely-reported observation by Lee Kuan Yew when he visited Boston International Airport in the United States and noticed that jets took off and landed over the sea, nearby minimising the noise for residents. Any extension to Paya Lebar would have worsened that situation for many thousands of Singaporeans. So the Changi move was a sound if expensive idea that proceeded for this and all the other good reasons.

As it was to be located at the coast, the new airport would be easily expandable through land reclamation. In addition, aircraft could fly over the sea, minimising the impact of noise and possible consequences on the ground in the event of an air mishap.

In June 1975, preparation work on the Changi site started with about 870 hectares of land being reclaimed, an area roughly the size of Sentosa

Island. Changi Airport was on its way to become one of the largest single development projects in Singapore's history[5]. To set the record in context, here's the airport's own development story:

Laying a strong foundation

Changi Airport's site, five times larger than the one at Paya Lebar, offered an opportunity to realise a bold vision for a modern airport, with room for expansion well into the future.

The lessons learnt from operating and managing Paya Lebar Airport were taken to heart.

Detailed studies of traffic flow patterns at major airports around the world were carefully scrutinised and analysed.

Facilities from runways to passenger and cargo terminals, baggage handling systems, office blocks, fuel supply and even car parks had to be carefully planned.

The foundation stone for Terminal 1 was laid in August 1979.

And planning and preparations for Changi's opening began one full year in advance to ensure a smooth and seamless transfer of operations from Paya Lebar. On 1 July 1981 the first flight, Singapore Airlines 101, touched down at Changi Airport at 0700 hours with 140 passengers from.

On opening day, the airport had 34 airlines operating 1200 scheduled flights each week connecting Singapore to 67 cities in 43 countries. Together, Changi and Paya Lebar registered 8.1 million passengers, 193,000 tonnes of air freight and 63,100 aircraft movements in 1981.

Growing from strength to strength

Four years after the opening of Terminal 1, construction work began on the second terminal and it was opened for operation in November 1990. Terminal 2 was built ahead of passenger demand to avoid congestion common in other airports around the region. Asia's first auto-guided people mover system was introduced to link Terminals 1 and 2.

Construction of Terminal 3 began in 2000 and it became operational on 9 January 2008. With the experience gained from the earlier terminals, Terminal 3 raised the bar further with its sophisticated architecture and modern eco-friendly design. The terminal increased the airport's maximum passenger capacity annually by 22 million, bringing the total annual capacity of Changi Airport to more than 70 million passengers.

Over the past three decades, CAG, previously part of the Civil Aviation Authority of Singapore (CAAS), had successfully established Changi Airport as the world's most awarded airport. With more than 370 accolades under its belt, Changi had come a long way since its humble beginnings in 1981, when Terminal 1 first opened.

One of the world's busiest international airports today, Changi Airport is regarded as a major air hub in Asia. It handled about 43 million passenger movements in FY10/11, serving about 100 airlines flying to some 200 cities in about 60 countries and territories worldwide. With over 70,000 square metres of commercial space across its four terminals, Changi Airport is also one of Singapore's best places for shopping and dining.

To spread the success of Changi Airport far and wide, CAG invests in and manages foreign airports through its subsidiary Changi Airports International (CAI). CAI's objective is to build a quality portfolio of airport investments worldwide with strong markets and significant development potential. Its key business activities include investments in airports, as well as the provision of consultancy and airport management services. Today, CAI's presence covers major economies including China, India, the Middle East, South America and Europe.

Changi Airports International (CAI) is both an investor and manager of airports worldwide.

The company is built on the expertise and resources of Singapore's Changi Airport. Since its inception in 1981, the airport has garnered more than 400 international awards testifying to its unrivalled standards of operational efficiency and passenger experience.

In 2011, CAI was conferred the Asia Pacific Airport Investment Company of the Year Award by global growth consulting firm Frost & Sullivan. It was the second time that CAI had won the award, the first being in 2008. ...CAI's investment philosophy is one which recognizes airports as a unique class of assets: a vital part of a country's transport infrastructure on which its economy, trade and business depend.

Mr Lim, known to keep a low profile and let others take the credit, did occasionally pop up in the media or through announcements. One of these rare "appearances" was in April 2011 when he oversaw the appointment of new CEO of Changi Airports International[6].

In the official report of the occasion: Mr Lim Chin Beng, Chairman of CAI, said, "We welcome Lim Liang Song to the Changi family. He brings with him invaluable experience in the area of aviation investments, including the development and management of a portfolio of aviation assets".

The Chairman of CAI was also on hand to thank Mr Wong Woon Hiong for his contributions to CAI.

Since Changi Airport's corporatisation in July 2009, Woon Liong has driven increased collaboration and alignment between CAI and CAG to further refine CAI's investment strategy. Under his leadership, CAI made key acquisitions with strategic investments in Bengal Aerotropolis Projects Ltd, a greenfield airport city project in Durgapur, India, and Gemina S.p.A., the holding company for Italy's largest airport group, Aeroporti di Roma.

He has also spearheaded the development of Changi's portfolio through CAI's consultancy and management services offered to overseas airports including in China, India, the Middle East and Europe. This includes a six-year management contract with Dammam Airport in Saudi Arabia, a milestone project for CAI.

The same Mr Wong, 59, had previously served as Director-General of the CAAS for 15 years before retiring in 2007. He was subsequently appointed to the CAG that year and assumed the position of CEO of CAI in August 2008.

Working together — the former head of Singapore Airlines Mr Lim and the former head of Civil Aviation in Singapore Mr Wong — had shown that wise and experienced men could continue to serve the country and promote the attributes of Changi Airport better than anyone. And not only help the airport win awards — it collected 410 between 1981 and 2012 — but also win business abroad to help other countries and cities build airports to challenge the best.

Endnotes

1. Changi Airport Group (Singapore) Pte Ltd (CAG) was formed on 16 June 2009 and the corporatisation of Changi Airport followed on 1 July 2009. As the airport company managing Changi Airport, CAG undertakes key functions focusing on airport operations and management, air hub development, commercial activities and airport emergency services. Through its subsidiary Changi Airports International, the Group invests in and manages foreign airports to spread the success of Changi Airport internationally. CAI also provides training services to overseas airports in areas such as airport commercial management, operational efficiency and customer service. Some training programmes are conducted, in collaboration with the Singapore Aviation Academy (SAA) and the China Singapore Aviation Management Academy (CSAMA).

2. Reference to *Business Traveller* presentation to SIA. Found at Changi Airport Group's press release on the award (18 September 2012), available at http://www.changiairportgroup. com/export/sites/caas/assets/media_release_2012/Media_Release_-_For_25th_timex_ Business_Traveller_names_Changi_Airport_worlds_best_xwebx.pdf.

3. A transcript of the speech by Mr Lim Boon Heng can be found at http://www.temasek. com.sg/mediacentre/speeches?detailid=18541

4. When it launched the CAG-Howe Yoon Chong (CAG-HYC) Book Prize, this from the media release: http://www.mynewsdesk.com/sg/singapore-changi-airport/pressreleases/ media-release-changi-airport-group-launches-book-prize-in-honour-of-mr-howe-yoon- chong-780546

5. Extract from article in the Changi Connection, available at http://www.changiairportgroup. com/export/sites/caas/assets/changi_connection/CAG-AR2011-Corp.pdf.

6. Mr Lim quotes from Changi Airport Group's press release (25 April 2011) available at http://www.changiairportgroup.com/export/sites/caas/assets/media_release_2011/25_ April_2011.pdf.

Touring Masters: Taking on the role of tourists for a change, Lim Chin Beng and son Arthur had the chance to play a round of golf at the Augusta National Golf Club, home of the US Masters Tournament. (Photo from the Lim family collection.)

"The pleasure we derive from journeys is perhaps dependent more on the mindset with which we travel than on the destination we travel to".

(Alain de Botton, *The Art of Travel*)

CHAPTER 18

TOURISM CHIEF

An award in 1990 for Singapore's "Outstanding Contribution to Tourism" could not have gone to a better man. But it was matched — in style and wit at least — by the presentation in the same year of a novel but well-conceived thank you scroll to Lim Chin Beng from Batey Ads.

Billing Mr Lim as "the brave lone ranger" for coming to rescue the tourist industry after the recession had hit all parts of the economy, the words of the scroll rang true:

> *Now business is booming but we've not forgotten*
>
> *Those years in the doldrums, when things were so rotten.*
>
> *All the hotels are full to the brim*
>
> *And we know it's all thanks to the man they called Lim.*

The advertising agency ended its glowing tribute by describing him as "the quiet achiever".

He was touched by this acknowledgment, just as he was pleased to be recognised by the State for his outstanding contribution to tourism over the five year period.

And it is true to say that all who have worked with Mr Lim — whether around a board table, in negotiations for traffic rights or jet purchases, or with management and staff of the airline at all levels — the label "quiet achiever" fits like a glove.

Never one to get flustered or angry, demanding or critical, Mr Lim tackled every job, issue or problem put in front of him with dignity, with determination and with thoroughness.

From 1985 to 1989, while still serving in what was seen as practically a full-time job as Deputy Chairman (and immediate past Managing Director) of SIA, Mr Lim took on the job as Chairman of the Board — then known as the Singapore Tourist Promotion Board (STPB), now it is simply Singapore Tourism Board (STB).

One would think there was a natural affinity between airline and tourism board and certainly Mr Lim made that work better than anyone could. But the tourist board had to work with other airlines too, just as SIA had to work with other Governments to be seen to be supporting their tourist interests.

So you could point to some divided loyalties. It helped that the STPB had an airline man, Joseph Chew, seconded to it as its full-time Managing Director.

There was much to be gained from SIA and STPB working together.

And in his reign — with sterling day to day support from a team of excellent administrators and promoters — he made sure it all worked seamlessly.

Besides Mr Chew there was Jenny Chua — a very able tourist promoter who went on to be Raffles Hotel General Manager after its makeover and other high profiles roles, as well as Pamelia Lee (married to Lee Kuan Yew's brother Freddy Lee) who was a driving force for the conservation and heritage attractions.

The Lim years saw some remarkable moves in tourism promotion which took Singapore to the top of the league. Here are just some of the things that happened on his watch:

- Mounted the world's first Tourism Consumer Price Index to show that Singapore was a "value for money" destination when perceptions were that it was getting expensive.

- Hosted the Miss Universe pageant which resulted in unprecedented global television and media coverage for Singapore and its attractions.
- Launched a billion dollar fund to develop and enhance Singapore conservation, heritage and landmark attractions.
- Set a target for Singapore to reach five million tourist arrivals by 1990, from 3.68 million in 1987.
- Singapore launched its first internationally co-ordinated public relations campaign in its major markets — United Kingdom, Germany, Australia/ New Zealand, and North America — on top of extra effort in ASEAN and North Asia.
- Promoting Singapore as the best place in Asia to hold business meetings, incentives, conferences and exhibitions.
- Giving unprecedented support and promotion for Singapore staging of major sporting, arts, cultural, shopping and aviation events.
- Mounting some of the best international advertising seen, using the same agency that had taken SIA to such international heights.
- Saving Raffles Hotel — which Mr Lim stated was seen at the time as the "jewel in the crown" for Singapore's tourism.

To answer queries — in the media and elsewhere — that Singapore was becoming an expensive place to visit, Mr Lim countered that it always represented value for money. But not to take his own word for it, he had the Board commission a comprehensive comparative study and produced the first Tourism Consumer Price Index in the world.

It was undertaken by respected international accounting firm Price Waterhouse Coopers in 1986/87 and provided STPB with some very useful and reliable data to show that Singapore was on a par with Kuala Lumpur (in Malaysia) for tourist costs — accommodation, local transport, sightseeing etc. — and less expensive than Hong Kong, Tokyo, Sydney, and New York, among others. There was also a comparative shopping study done to compare a basket of goods purchased in a number of Asian cities.

Elevating Singapore's attractiveness as a destination was just part of the game plan for Mr Lim. He also elevated the tourism industry as a serious contributor to the economy.

This not only benefitted Singapore, but the ASEAN region and the wider Asia Pacific.

In a speech on International Tourism and the Asia Pacific Region delivered to the Chartered Institute of Transport Pacific Conference in June 1988, he made it clear that international tourism growth and airline development go hand in hand[1].

> *The objective of a tourist board and an airline may differ, but the ends and achievements are inter-dependent. One cannot operate effectively without the other.*

He reflected that a tourist destination cannot develop without the provision of regular and convenient air services. But likewise an airline cannot expect to fill its seats to new destinations, unless the country, island or resort "provides the necessary infrastructure and promotional backup to draw tourists and meet their needs on the ground".

Through his hands-on involvement in running an international airline and overseeing Singapore tourist promotional efforts, Mr Lim was well qualified to make some astute and profound observations of the importance of tourism for all, even beyond Singapore's shores.

He told the gathered transport industry delegates from throughout the Asia Pacific region that "every nation which wants to establish a viable tourist industry sees many economic advantages".

> *Tourists bring in foreign exchange of course, but more than that — a destination with tourist appeal can attract foreign investment for the development of airports, hotels and related facilities. Investment means jobs in the short term and longer term.*

He gave an overview of the growth forecasts of tourism globally: in 1987 the World Tourism Organisation (WTO) put tourist arrivals at 355 million — a new world record — and the Asia Pacific region distinguished itself as the fastest growing both in terms of tourist arrivals and receipts.

In 1987 there were 34 million international arrivals, an increase of 13.8% over 1986 — or a 69% growth in the five year period since 1982.

Money-wise, that meant US$18,500 million in tourism receipts for the region, an improvement of 28% over 1986 and 92% since 1982[2].

Besides Singapore, the other Asian countries to gain most — and experience double digit growth — were Hong Kong, Thailand, South Korea and Taiwan.

For Singapore, Mr Lim describes the growth "modest" in 1986 at 5.3% and a big jump of 15.3% growth of 3.68 million in 1987.

Of course, he would not even attempt to take any credit for this, but wisely points to forecasts to show that Singapore, along with other Asia Pacific countries, would continue to gain from the concurrent growth in travel — intra regional and inter-continental — as well as from air traffic, which Boeing predicted then would became the world's biggest aviation market in a few short years.

There is little doubt that tourism is well on the way to becoming the world's biggest business, Mr Lim pointed out. "Some would say it is that already. In the travel industry world yearbook, when they add up domestic and international tourism spending for 1987 they get to the figure of S$2 trillion".

Rosy as the picture was portrayed by Mr Lim at the time — 1988 remember — he was only cautiously optimistic, as he also made clear a number of constraints which could impact the business of tourism, if not taken into account.

> *Tourism and air travel are very sensitive to upheavals, like dramatic price hikes in oil or an outbreak of terrorism or some dreaded disease. Those we cannot predict. But what we can do is seek to remove some of the constraints we do have more control over.*

He saw the key constraints — for Singapore and the region — as follows:

- Distance from major markets is an inhibiting factor, which can be helped by use of faster aircraft and more direct services. "There needs to be more of a multi-destinational approach to long haul travel promotion".
- Shortage of airline capacity, which was already starting to make its presence felt for intra-regional travel and some long haul routes.

- Travel restrictions, as some Governments "feel the need to impose restrictions on outbound travel". He noted that some countries were coming to realise that the tourist industry depends on a free flow of people — inbound and outboard.
- Shortage of skilled manpower, as any industry which "grows so fast, you can expect a problem equipping with qualified people". There should be more developments to upgrade the range of training available to the whole industry.
- The vast over-water expanse that the region is noted for means more dependence on air travel to cover the distances. "It calls for more direct air services within the region to cater for specific travel needs of the sophisticated tourist".

As if to demonstrate that this quiet achiever (an economist by training) was thinking of more than numbers and dollars, he also set out — both for anyone he dealt with in the airline and the board — as well as to the audience of transport industry professionals experts in 1988, what he saw as five factors which were relevant to the development of tourism in this region.

He reiterated the importance of the **economic** factor and the **manpower** factor, but made it clear that the **cultural** factor and the **exotic** factor were equally important.

> We must always be conscious of the cultural and social implications of tourism developments. Tourism can and must contribute to and enhance a culture.

> As more and more people travel they will crave for more exoticism and excitement. We must always be coming up with new destinations, new attractions, new adventures to whet the appetites of the traveller.

But this visionary reserved his final point to the **accessibility** factor as it brings together his tourist industry focus with that of the airline, which he had driven to such international heights:

> As airlines access and tourist growth go hand-in-hand, the industry must seek to bring down the barriers to travel. Whether they

be restrictions on outgoing residents, to restrictions on airline capacity growth through air traffic agreements (or disagreements), the industry as a whole, and the economies of the countries, suffer.

This would not be Mr Lim's final word on tourist development or airline traffic rights, but they demonstrate both his commitment to the principles of "freedom of the skies" but also the untold benefits — cultural, economic and social — that travel and tourism brings to everyone on earth.

Endnotes

1. A number of references in this chapter come from the speech delivered by Mr Lim in 1988 and is in the author's own archive collection from his time when he worked as a consultant at STPB.

2. To put some perspective on both tourism statistics and the projections Mr Lim referred to in his 1988 speech, here is the latest (in January 2014) from the UN World Tourism Organisation: International tourist arrivals grew by 5% in 2013, reaching a record 1,087 million arrivals. Despite global economic challenges, international tourism results were well above expectations, with an additional 52 million international tourists travelling the world in 2013. For 2014, UNWTO forecasts 4% to 4.5% growth — again, above the long term projections. Available at http://dtxtq4w60xqpw.cloudfront.net/sites/all/files/pdf/unwto_highlights14_en_0.pdf.

High Fliers: Jimmy Lau, Ho Ching (CEO of Temasek Holdings and wife of the Prime Minister), Lee Hsien Loong and Lim Chin Beng, at the opening of the first Singapore Airshow in February 2008, at the new Changi location. (Photo by Experia Events.)

"There is a thrill of vulnerability at all airshows. There is no way of making everything completely safe. When the machines are being thrashed to capacity and the pilots are flying at their limits to dazzle, things are bound to go wrong sometimes. There have been some historic disasters, but the danger is a part of the attraction".

(Alex James, bass player of the group Blur and a private pilot, 2007)

CHAPTER 19

AEROSPACE SHOWCASE

Not a showman himself, but Lim Chin Beng has been credited with putting Singapore on the global map with the best airshow in Asia and staging what is regarded as the third biggest and best aerospace showcase after Farnborough and Paris.

It all started with a relatively small but never-the-less international show of strength at the old Paya Lebar location in September 1981, soon after the international airport had moved to Changi. Then, early in 1984, it was held in and around converted hangars in the old air base area opposite Changi's terminal. By 1986 it had grown into an even bigger and better show with the rather grand official title of Asian Aerospace.

Singapore Airlines was a keen participant, as was the Singapore Government, the military and the country's Government owned aviation engineering services.

Keen to see the show grow in stature and business importance, Mr Lim had actively promoted the event, and eventually took on the role of Chairman of Asian Aerospace in 1998. It was a delicate balancing act, along with his other jobs in the public and private sector, once he returned from Japan and had relinquished his SIA directorship.

Jimmy Lau — the man who had worked with Lim Chin Beng over the years by tapping his contacts and connections for many exhibitions including tourism and aviation shows, says his chairman was once again the "quiet achiever" who connected so well with Government, airline and aviation bosses around the world, as well as made sure the Singapore military and industry participants were fully in the picture. A diplomat at work. A man on a mission. A man who never took no for an answer.

And when troubles arose with the Asian Aerospace event organiser Reed Exhibitions a few years later — Jimmy moved on and so did Mr Lim — masterfully handling the demise of one very successful event and introducing a new one, Singapore Airshow, that could be totally managed from within and would go on to be as successful, if not more so, than its predecessor.

At the heart of it all, the touch of class and aerospace pedigree, epitomised by Lim Chin Beng and the Singapore institutions he represented, past and present.

In typical understatement, which he was known for, this is how he welcomed delegates to the 2008 event in his message in the official programme — the first at the new location[1]:

> *As someone who has been closely involved in the development of Singapore's aviation industry, it has been a very great pleasure for me to oversee the launch of Singapore Airshow, and to welcome delegates and exhibitors to the inaugural event.*

The selected venue for the permanent site was situated on a plot of reclaimed land just beyond the northern edge perimeter fencing of Changi Air Base, which was itself located due east of the nearby Singapore Changi Airport. It allowed for aircraft access from Changi's existing airfields but also has a new strip of its own to minimise disruption to the steady flow of normal commercial traffic.

This would be as good a place as any to record Singapore's history of involvement in staging aviation and aerospace events. As this book has "Fly Past" incorporated in its title, it is certainly appropriate to show that the strategically located island played a crucial role in the early days of flight and Singaporeans — before taking to the skies themselves — certainly welcomed with open arms the first aviators.

While Mr Lim was not around for the first few of these "airshows", he certainly played a crucial role in many of them later — as interested observer and/or active participant — from the time of his first airline job in 1960 to the present day.

Let's take a chronological journey "back to the future":

1911

For Singapore, the very first "show" by an aviator was back in 1911 when Belgian pilot Joseph Christiaens flew in his Bristol Boxkite biplane at Farrer Park Racecourse in 16 March 1911. One could also say that this was in effect, the beginning of Singapore's involvement in aviation.

When you consider this was a mere eight years since the Wright brothers memorable first flight at Kitty Hawk in 17 December 1903, Singapore was introduced to the joys and challenges of aviation very early on. There were many flying demonstrations since and, according to Goh Yong Kiat in *Where Lions Fly*, other occasions which involved a fly past of more than one aircraft which could be more accurately described as an airshow[2].

1937

The opening ceremony of Kallang Airport in 12 June 1937 was a real "show time" and Goh's book features many images and words, showing a fly past of many aircraft, old and new at the time, and an array of aircraft on static display for thousands to see. While the World War years and Singapore's occupation by the Japanese, interrupted the civilian side of things significantly, remarkably a lot of air field construction went on which gave Singapore more sealed landing and take-off space.

1948

But it was at the same location in September 1948 when Singapore held what was described as its first "Air Day". Another Air Day was held in 1949, but the records say little or nothing of aviation events of the 1950s.

1961

What was headlined as the "First International Air Show" was held on 8–16 April in 1961 at Paya Lebar Airport. The airshow was described as "an unqualified success and attracted much favourable publicity for Singapore". As this was the year after Mr Lim took his first job in the airline business, his employer Malayan Airways was certainly on show as this was the airline's key airport location. He was one of many thousands who took in the event, which was a real preview of the role Singapore would play in becoming a regional centre for the operation of global airlines.

1963

To mark the Federation of Malaysia, which Singapore became part of, there was a three-day airshow of strength at Paya Lebar. Then and ever since, Singapore has been attracting aircraft of all sorts, their manufacturers, and buyers — whether looking for commercial or military equipment — and Mr Lim was never very far from the action in the air and on the ground.

1965

There was an opening of a new passenger terminal at Paya Lebar that year and while the commercial aircraft and airlines were well represented, what captured the public's attention was an impressive aerial display by aircraft of the RAF and RAAF visiting for the occasion. This was the year Singapore came into its own as a nation and showed that aviation would be one of the economic drivers. By the end of that year, aircraft movements at the nation's gateway reached 47,551. Plenty of aircraft to see in the sky and on the ground.

1969

As if to reinforce Singapore's strategic aviation location, the England to Australia air race positioned through Singapore in December that year and everyone who wanted to got a good look at many of the 70 aircraft from 16 countries which had managed to make it this far on the marathon journey. It was an important year for Singapore in more ways than one. The Government-designated Seletar Airfield was identified as a "revenue earning and developing facility", and this heralded the "birth of an aircraft industry".

1972

Even before SIA got off the ground with its own distinctly branded jets in this momentous and historic year for Singapore's aerospace business, the British-French jointly built supersonic Concorde paid a visit to Paya Lebar and few could miss its distinct look and sound. In June, Singaporeans were also treated to another aerial show from its very own Singapore Air Defence Command (SADC) military aircraft at and over the Changi Air Base.

1975

When the SADC changed its name to Republic of Singapore Air Force (RSAF) it was occasion enough to take to the air with a precision fly past which showed Singapore military flying machines over the air base and over the city. It was also the start of a tradition where military aircraft put on a birthday fly past for National Day every year.

1976

Singapore shared its aerospace expertise around when in April it took part in the three day ASEAN Air Rally held in Indonesia.

1977

This was an important year for SIA, as it marked the 30th anniversary of its beginnings (as Malayan Airways which started at Kalang Airport), so it put on an open house at its new hangar for 747s at Paya Lebar on 7 May. It allowed a large percentage of the 100,000 who came to the event to walk through the jumbo jet on show. In September of the same year, when SIA took delivery of its first Boeing 727 aircraft, one put on a fly past of its own on 15 September, followed by two more arrivals in October (and another two the next year). But even more impressive — in size, shape and sound — was the return of the Concorde, this time on 9 December, sporting SIA's distinctive livery on one side at the start of an "irregular" supersonic service between London and Singapore.

1981

To mark Singapore's very special aviation year of events — the opening of Changi's new international airport — Asian Aerospace had its inauguration at the vacated Paya Lebar airport, which was to become the home for military operations. Held from 23–27 September 1981, it was acknowledged as the "first Asian Aerospace", drawing top aviation personnel and authorities from ASEAN countries and experts from around the world.

It was organised by Industrial and Trade Fairs Ltd and fully sponsored by the Economic Development Board (EDB), which hoped the exhibition would boost Singapore's image as an aerospace centre, especially with the opening of Changi Airport. The event demonstrated a very impressive beginning for an international airshow and at least one visiting overseas journalist can vouch for that[3].

For the record, the 1981 airshow occupied some 10,000 square metres of floor space, featuring the latest in commercial and private aircraft, avionics, engines and equipment at stands of some 120 companies. The organisers managed to attract the participation of renowned international aircraft manufacturers such as Boeing, McDonnell Douglas, Fokker, Cessna and Aerospatiale.

Described as "modest by European and American standards", partly because of rules prohibiting exhibitions of a military character, there was a static display of 12 business jets, light planes and helicopters with an interest item of a 1940-vinate Boeing Stearman biplane. Flying demonstrations were limited to two helicopters (the MBB Bo-105 made by Nurianto and the Aerospatiale AS350B Ecureuil) and an Ayres Turbo Thrust agricultural aircraft.

Setting the standard for future events, the five day exhibition also included conferences on aviation matters, designed to encourage aviation and aero-engineering industry authorities from around the world to meet and hold discussions in Singapore. Records show that "a total of 4000 local and overseas trade visitors attended the airshow during the three days allocated to the trade, while an estimated 100,000 members of the public visited it during the last two days".

1984

The second Asian Aerospace exhibition would begin to feature military aerospace technology, and the size of the show would increase by more than one and half times. In the years to come, true to the ambitions of EDB, the Asian Aerospace airshow would grow to become a major international aviation event.

Flight Show Daily editor Hugh McAtear reminded readers that in his first interview with Lim Chin Beng during Asian Aerospace '84, the airline boss sent out a warning of slower growth than the meteoric expansion experienced in the preceding years. His statement was a New Year message to the staff of Singapore Airlines, in his capacity as Deputy Chairman of the Republic's flag carrier[4].

1986

This year was not only the third Asian Aerospace but it was the first under the official Asian Aerospace Pte Ltd company formed by Singapore Aircraft Industries (SAI) — which had itself been formed in 1983 to bring together all parts of the nation's aerospace industries — and Reed Exhibitions as a joint venture to run the show.

1988

There was a new location at the northern end of Changi's runway one for the fourth Asian Aerospace, including buildings and plenty of accessible aircraft display space. It was rather grandly called Singapore International Exhibition and Convention Centre.

1990

The beginning of the 1990s saw Singapore advancing its aerospace business with a noted shift towards diversification and globalisation. Spearheading this was the biennial Asian Aerospace exhibition and its associated conferences, which as they grew in size and scope, would attract an increasing number of multinational exhibitors and participants. Mr Goh records, in his excellent survey of aviation over the years, that although other air shows were sprouting up all over the region — Langkawi, Beijing, Taipei and Tokyo — the Singapore event "remained the most prominent".

1992

This year the event was marked by significant participation by the Russians and also saw an increased focus on Asian airport equipment and technology exhibits. The first issue of the show daily — *Flight Daily News* — on 25 February 1992 records that Asian Aerospace's future is assured, dispelling any rumours that the show would move anywhere[5]. Also reported was an "Asia Pacific air traffic upsurge" by International Air Transport Association's (IATA) Director General Dr Gunter O. Eser and that Airbus A340 would be making its world debut at the Changi show.

1994

The seventh airshow, with the expanded title of Asian Aerospace and Defence Technology Exhibition and Airshow was staged from 22 to 27 February. It took place — according to the aviation chronicler Mr Goh — in an "atmosphere of gloom". He noted that while the west was in recession, "the continued growth of aviation in Asia meant that Changi was the best place for to be for those serious about staying in the business".

The Singapore show actually surpassed its 1992 performance with more than 900 firms representing 36 countries. The event's Media Centre also looked after more than 1000 media representatives — reporters, editors, photographers and camera crew — covering the event for more than 400 media organisations around the world[6].

1996

This was one airshow which seemed to go against the flow in the global aerospace industry and maintain its reputation as the place to be to not only see — on the ground and in the air — the latest and the best, but also to witness some big deals. This year at Asian Aerospace, SIA and GE Capital both inked record breaking orders with Boeing. SIA committed to a US$12.7 billion order while GE Capital signed off on US$11.6 billion.

1998

When Lim Chin Beng was called on to be Chairman of Asian Aerospace in advance of the 1998 event, he was interviewed for the *Flight Show Daily* by Hugh McAtear. Mr Lim looks to what the future holds for the industry and world's third largest aerospace exhibition[7]:

> *It's not an ideal time to hold a major exhibition in light of the regional financial turmoil, concedes Lim Chin Beng, but it's not as if you can just move such an event on the calendar to a more suitable time.*
>
> *For this show, the organisers expect 10% fewer visitors than attended the last event, but this will translate into around 25,000; a figure which Lim says is still regarded as healthy.*
>
> *There is hardly an industry in the region or internationally that remains unaffected by the Asian currency crisis, and Lim says the organisers are happy that many exhibitors have still supported the show as an indication of their long-term confidence in the region, and in the show itself.*
>
> *The joint-venture partners in Asian Aerospace, Reed Exhibition Companies and Singapore Technologies Aerospace, have signalled their commitment to the event with the recent 20-year deal to organise the show well into the next century.*
>
> *The inbound chairman pays a tribute to his predecessor, Colonel Quek Poh Huat, for the successful development of Asian Aerospace as the region's premier aerospace showcase.*
>
> *"As far as the industry is concerned attendance at Asian Aerospace is a must — that is a tribute to all the hard work which has gone into the event."*
>
> *Lim says he looks forward optimistically to the future. Knowing full well the cyclical nature of business from his extensive airline experience, he adds: "Singapore's location and infrastructure has always been a major selling point for the show. We have to make sure we continue to provide the facilities which our customers demand.*

"We see a continued trend towards mergers and alliances, and attendance at this event has proven to be a key factor in providing companies with the business contacts they need to make these alliances a reality".

"As far as the industry is concerned attendance at Asian Aerospace is a must", says Lim Chin Beng.

2000

For this event, marking the start of a new millennia, Tom Ballantyne, an aviation writer and editor with a long track record, wrote this about Asian Aerospace for Orient Aviation magazine[8]:

> *Deals worth more than US$3 billion were clinched by participants at the recent Asian Aerospace 2000 in Singapore, making it one of the most successful air shows on record. That figure is expected to soar higher as on-going negotiations firm up.*
>
> *This adds up to the air show being a major fillip for the region's aviation industry as it emerges from troubled economic times. While analysts continue to preach caution and warn it is too soon for over-optimism, there seemed to be hardly a cloud on the horizon as major manufacturers unanimously forecast good times ahead.*
>
> *Rolls-Royce's indefatigable chairman, Sir Ralph Robins, announced business worth nearly half a billion dollars for engines to power 100 Embraer regional jets.*
>
> *Indeed, Rolls-Royce is increasing its presence in Singapore to manage its expanding regional business. Sir Ralph forecast the number of staff employed by his company in the island state would increase from 10 to as many as 400 within three years.*
>
> *The Asia-Pacific currently accounts for a third of Rolls-Royce's firm order book, worth US$22.5 billion, for commercial aircraft engines.*

The Orient Aviation report also noted that Jimmy Lau, Managing Director of Asian Aerospace, disclosed the exhibition's planned move to a new purpose-built site has been deferred from 2002 to 2004. "The site is on reclaimed land alongside what will be the third runway at Changi Airport. It has been decided a longer period is needed for proper land settlement", he explained.

2002

Despite the tough time the international aviation went through after the 9/11 terrorist attack in New York, Asian Aerospace 2002 attracted a significant number of exhibiting companies — 747 — from 36 countries including 70 of the top 100 aerospace companies. For the record, 23,433 trade visitors from 78 countries and 60,000 public visitors, even though there was no high powered aerial displays to enjoy this year. The new location for the airshow was not ready and exhibitors and attendees would have to wait another six years for the move to take place from the familiar if rather cramped Changi site.

2004

In February that year Asian Aerospace maintained its high standards and it boasted 759 exhibiting companies from 37 countries, a total of 26,814 trade visitors from 81 countries recorded, and trade deals amounting to USD3.52 billion were concluded.

2006

It was a high benchmark which had been set for airshows, but every year Asian Aerospace seemed to hit it or exceed the record set before. The largest edition of the show ever held was the 2006 event — the last at the old venue at the end of Changi Airport runway one.

It was to be the 13th and final show under the Asian Aerospace branding in Singapore. Held jointly with several conferences including the Asia Pacific Security Conference (APSEC), the C4I Asia Conference (C4i Asia), the Asia Pacific Airline Training Symposium (APATS), the Asian Aerospace UAV Asia-Pacific Conference and the IATA/Asian Aerospace Aviation Summit, also featuring a rebranded Asian Defence Technology military component. At show's end, it drew 940 exhibitors from 43 countries, 34,300 trade participants from 89 countries and concluded a record US$15.2 billion in sales.

2008

Occupying its new site for the first time was the Singapore Airshow 2008 — a new name but standing firmly on the strength and reputation of its predecessor — it was here that Mr Lim did his honours as Chairman of the event organising team.

The new site boasted 40,000 square metres of fully air-conditioned exhibition space, 2,000 parking lots for trade visitors and motorists as well as 100,000 square metres of outdoor space for exhibitions and functions. It was promptly named as the Changi Exhibition Centre to set it apart from the Changi International Exhibition and Convention Centre which had been in use by its predecessor, the Asian Aerospace exhibitions, from 1988 to 2006.

Mr Lim had more than one VIP on hand the day of the show's opening when he took to the podium to welcome not only Singapore's Prime Minister Lee Hsien Loong, but a few more heads of state, ministers, military personnel from the region and a host of aircraft manufacturers, suppliers and delegates.

It is with great pleasure that I welcome you to the official opening of the first Singapore Airshow, the largest aviation and aerospace exhibition ever held in the Asia Pacific region.

When we announced our plans to hold this all-new event, back in 2006, we had a clear vision of what we wanted to achieve. Today, that vision has become a reality. Just two years ago, the spot where you are now was an empty landfill site. Today, we see a purpose-built, 40,000 square metre exhibition hall which is a fitting and permanent home for the Singapore Airshow, an event which we hope and believe will create a new standard for the aviation industry.

It is not simply a question of size or scale. When we started planning for this event, we took extensive feedback from exhibitors, guests and airshow veterans from across the industry. We wanted to know what they expected, and — in particular — their most common dislikes and frustrations. We heard about traffic jams, long queues for registration, intrusive security, lack of business facilities, not enough food and beverage outlets.

One of the advantages of starting with a clean sheet of paper is that it allowed us to focus on the needs of exhibitors and guests, and we have done our best to ensure that the Singapore Airshow is the most convenient and efficient place to do business on the global airshow circuit.

I'm sure you will have noticed the new six-lane access road which links the airshow site to Changi Coast Road; the e-ticketing booths at the registration gateway and the plasma screens which allow us to adjust the security lines and minimise hold-ups. You may not realise our guest passes also contain RFID tags which allow us to monitor traffic flows around the exhibition hall, so we can spot potential bottlenecks.

We've deliberately made the aisles wider than normal, so there is enough space to accommodate guests in comfort — and of course, given Singapore's climate, we have ensured that the exhibition hall is fully air-conditioned.

On that note, I should say that one of the most common sights at international conferences and exhibitions here in Singapore is foreign business executives struggling with heavy, formal suits which would be perfectly comfortable in Europe or North America, but which were not designed for the heat and humidity of Southeast Asia. So, we have made this the first major airshow with a "smart casual" dress code. We really hope our overseas guests feel free to abandon their suits and ties, because we would like you to do business in comfort here at the Singapore Airshow.

The achievement of our vision would not have been possible without the tremendous hard work of the show team, and the support of our partners in the Civil Aviation Authority of Singapore and the Defence Science and Technology Agency. Above all, it would not have been possible without the support and commitment of our exhibitors and industry partners from around the world.

I am proud to say that more than 800 exhibitors from 42 countries are here at the first Singapore Airshow, representing almost every *major industry player from the civil, military, general aviation sectors. Over the next few days, we will see more than 30,000 trade visitors passing through the exhibition hall, not forgetting more than 50,000 aviation enthusiasts who will flock to the site on the public days next Saturday and Sunday.*

Mr Lim concluded his address by acknowledging the show's VIP visitors which included three Heads of State, ten Ministers of Transport, 12 Ministers of Defence, 21 airline CEOs, the heads of the two major international industry bodies, ICAO and IATA, and high-level government delegations from more than 30 countries.

"This truly is the only place to be for manufacturers, suppliers, buyers, operators and decision-makers — in fact for anyone who is serious about doing business in the world's fastest-growing aviation market," said Mr Lim.

What he did not say, but most in the industry knew that this was how Singapore was showing it was going it alone, moving away from its association with long time exhibition organising partner, after what was described as "disagreements between co-organisers Reed Exhibitions and Singapore Technologies in 2006 forced its relocation from 2007".

While it reaffirmed the aviation and commercial rivalry between Hong Kong — which was chosen as the location for the re-invented Asian Aerospace — Singapore made sure it kept up the standard and attendance and business of past events. As there was a lot banking on the 2008 show, headed by Mr Lim, it was pleasing that the industry declared it a success.

With the first four days reserved for trade visitors at the purpose-built Changi Exhibition Centre, the event saw the return of aerobatic flying displays put on by the Black Knights of the Republic of Singapore Air Force and the Roulettes of the Royal Australian Air Force. Also held concurrently are several seminars and conferences, including the Singapore Airshow Aviation Leadership Summit, the Global Air Power Conference, the International Defence Procurement Conference, the C4I Asia Conference and the Global Space and Technology Convention. The static displays included several themed exhibition pavilions, including the Airport Pavilion and the Integrated Land Defence Pavilion. The ATW Airline Industry Achievement Awards was also held during the Airshow.

2010

After the first of the "new" Singapore Airshows, the standard had to be maintained and in 2010, it featured more than 800 exhibiting companies from over 40 countries. More than 60 of the top 100 global aerospace companies participated, including Boeing, EADS, Honeywell, Lockheed Martin, Northrop Grumman and Rolls-Royce. Mitsubishi Aircraft, Liebherr-Aerospace, B/E Aerospace and a number of Asian aerospace firms made their first appearances at the show. The show hosted 20 country pavilions, with Switzerland, New Zealand, Russia and Romania making their inaugural presence.

2012

Two years later, with its theme, "Big Show, Big Opportunities", Singapore Airshow 2012 was held from 14 to 19 February 2012 and hosted nearly 900 exhibitors from 50 countries, such as Boeing, Airbus, Embraer, and Bombardier. Fully half of the exhibitors represented the defence industry, but representation by the business aviation section grew significantly, including private jet manufacturers Gulfstream, Bombardier and Embraer, in response to rising demand from Asia's growing class of super-rich. The 2012 event also hosted the Aviation Leadership Summit.

2014

Coming to the current year, with Mr Lim no longer there as Chairman — he was replaced by Tan Pheng Hock as Chairman of the organiser Experia Events — the cast had been set. Singapore Airshow 2014 wrapped up the trade segment of the six-day event with deals announced worth US$32 billion (+3% versus 2012), and both participating companies (1018 or +13% versus 2012) and trade attendees (45,152 or +1% versus 2012) exceeded the 2012 totals!

Major contracts were announced for Airbus, Embraer, Boeing, Rolls-Royce, ATR, Pratt & Whitney, GE Capital Aviation Services, Bombardier, CFM International, Augusta Westland, Rockwell Collins, ST Engineering, Turbomeca and many more. For the organizers, this reinforced Singapore Airshow's standing as the must-attend and must-exhibit show on the worldwide Airshow circuit for both military and commercial aviation.

Maintaining such a high level of event as well as exhibitors and delegates had been a key role of Mr Lim's, right hand man — Jimmy Lau — for many years. He announced that the 2014 event would be his last.

It was also an occasion where the environmental impact of aviation was not only discussed in detail but aircraft manufacturers were demonstrating that they had got the message. They were making lighter weight, more fuel efficient aircraft, and at the associated IATA conference, important speakers from far and wide were saying what the industry had to do to cut its emissions before it was forced to do so, as the Europeans, had already tried to enforce[9].

Mr Lim admits that while the environmental impact involved in operating an airline was not on the agenda when he was in the most senior management role, SIA led the industry by taking steps to save fuel and running costs by buying and operating the most modern fleet in the world. Since his days in the airline business, SIA has made some impressive moves to go further and reinforcing its commitment to efficiency and sustainability[10].

Singapore Airlines embraces new technology from aircraft and engine manufacturers. We often order new aircraft types before they're built, because we believe in backing manufacturers to develop innovative technology. As such, the airline operates one of the youngest and most fuel-efficient fleets in the skies.

We also take pride in being the first to operate the Airbus A380, the cleanest and greenest aircraft in operation today. Its fuel burn per seat mile and carbon dioxide emissions per customer are the lowest of any aircraft. The A380 is also quieter, both inside and outside the cabin.

On the ground, the airline continues to do its part for the environment by implementing electronic ticketing across its network — an initiative that not only reduces costs but saves trees as well — and embraces energy conservation and green building designs at the workplace to reduce energy usage.

For Mr Lim, the continued strong performance of the nation's airline, airport and aerospace industry was reflected in the show itself. It demonstrated every two years not only the best of the best from around the world, but the growth of a home-grown aerospace industry that could match anything in the Asia Pacific and rival those of much bigger centres of excellence in Europe and America.

And while he would admit in 2008 that he was "someone who has been closely involved in the development of Singapore's aviation industry", few of the industry observers knew how much this involvement entailed.

Here was the same man who had headed Singapore Airlines and had direct involvement in the airline for 36 years, he had also been Chairman of the Tourist Board — promoting events like this around the world — and had the important role of Chairman of ST Aerospace, as the premier aircraft servicing organisation in Singapore and Chairman of Changi Airports International, selling the "wares" of Changi and its expertise.

The new Singapore Airshow was more than a worthy successor to the Asian Aerospace because of the people involved in its management and the backing it had from key Government agencies and private sector businesses. Lim Chin Beng and Jimmy Lau together headed a formidable team that made sure Singapore maintained its position as the premier place in Asia for the best of aerospace events.

Endnotes

1. This information as well as more on airshows past and present from Experia Events, who have managed the Singapore Airshow at its new Changi venue since 2008. Their official website is www.experiaevents.com.

2. This and a lot of other relevant events and dates come from the excellent history of Singapore's aviation from 1911 to 2011 in *Where Lions Fly* by Goh Yong Kiat, Singapore premiere aerospace historian. Having grown up with a passion for things that fly, Yong Kiat joined the RSAF in 1979 as a technician. He soon became an air engineering officer (AEO) and served in various staff and command positions. In 2002 he joined ST Aerospace where he was involved in the company's MRO business, as well as air charter services and aviation training. He is currently (in 2014) an executive vice president for ST Aerospace for aviation and training services, and also for the company's defence business. More information at www.ainonline.com.

3. The author visited Singapore on an Air New Zealand inaugural flight to mark the opening of Changi Airport that year and visited Paya Lebar to witness the indoor and outdoor display of the very first Asian Aerospace. He also attended the 1984 event at Changi Airport and many of them since.

4. Hugh McAtear's reference to Lim Chin Beng and the 1984 Asian Aerospace is available at http://www.flightglobal.com/news/articles/asian-aerospace-sees-clear-skies-beyond-the-turbulence-33170/.

5. Physical copy of the *Flight Daily News* for Asian Aerospace 1992 (in the author's possession as he was a contributor to the show newspaper at the time.)

6. The author has a so-far unpublished record of his attendance and involvement at many airshows in Singapore and elsewhere. His company, Hickson Public Relations, was hired by the organisers to promote Asian Aerospace 1994 to the world and to manage the media centre for the event itself. He has also represented and supported various clients — including Lockheed Martin, BMW Rolls Royce and DHL — to maximise their involvement at the shows.

7. Hugh McAtear's interview with Lim Chin Beng for *Flight Daily News* in 1998.

8. "AA 2000 reflects regional recovery", by Tom Ballantyne (April 2000), *Orient Aviation*. Available at http://www.orientaviation.com/section.php?currenyIssue=I20080731220733-x74sN&currentSection=news&currentArticle=A20080801130859-lWepp&.

9. The author wrote this article for his ABC Carbon Express summing up the discussions at the associated Singapore Airshow conference and covering plans to deal with carbon emissions from the aviation industry. It also published online by Ana Shell Media, available at http://anashell.com/anashell/2014/03/11/blue-skies-ahead-greener-flights/.

10. Singapore Airlines' Commitment to the Environment. Available at http://www.singaporeair.com/en_UK/about-us/sia-history/sia-environment/.

Joining Forces: Singapore Airlines showing off its Star Alliance allegiance at Changi Airport with other aircraft sporting the regular SIA livery. (Photo by Sim Kok Chwee from the Singapore Airlines collection).

"Like marriages, business alliances involve people. People can be trusting, optimistic and tolerant, but also weak, overbearing and devious. Larger-than-life personalities plighting their troth and looking towards a bright tomorrow rarely feature. It's not very romantic. But business partnerships would be more durable if the joys of the partnering part were offset more frequently by the realities of the business bit".

(By Andrew Hill, the management editor of the *Financial Times*, 2011)

CHAPTER 20

AVIATION ALLIANCES

W hile it might not be Lim Chin Beng's choice of words, the airline he managed often had a love-hate relationship with other airlines.

Admiring on occasions, ruthlessly antagonistic at times, the international airline business is not a cosy community, where bosses rub shoulders and pat each other's backs. Which is why, from the beginning, SIA was never comfortable about belonging to the IATA club — the International Air Transport Association. It appeared to want everyone to not only play by the same rules, but follow the same very restrictive practices regarding how much to charge for a fare and what you could serve on board.

SIA was consequently the first airline in the world to openly serve alcoholic drinks to economy class travellers for free, as well as provide headphones as part of the ticket price.

But eventually SIA did relent, not to give in to the uncompetitive ways of the airline club, but because IATA changed its rules to make it possible for airlines like SIA to treat its passengers in the way it wanted to — and at the right price.

SIA also not only learned to live with some of its very competitive — even combative — airlines, like Lufthansa and Air New Zealand. It ended up getting into the same bed!

Yes, the two highly competitive carriers were among the early members of another club — the Star Alliance. Lufthansa, a founding member in 1997, while Air New Zealanel joined in 1999. SIA joined in April 2000 and also took a stake in Air New Zealand which turned out to be something of a disaster.

Airlines come and go. And so do alliances. Some start as partnerships and collaborations in the volatile world of aviation. So SIA has had its share of enjoying — or otherwise — the ins and outs of alliances and partnerships. Choosing who to work with and share the marketplace with.

In the days when Mr Lim was running the airline, he saw some significant linkups. Before then, in the Malayan Airways days, BOAC — which later became British Airways — and Qantas, were co-owners of SIA's predecessor. So he knew from early times the value and the obligations of airline partnerships.

But the key alliance Mr Lim was intimately aware of and worked with, which showed signs of having some significant benefits, was the tie up with Swissair in Europe and Delta in the United States.

It might have had some code share agreements before then, but it was not until 1989 when SIA went into a tri-partite alliance with Swissair and Delta. But the partnership was terminated ten years later and after divesting their 5% stake in each other's airline.

Did it live up to expectations? It could have evolved into a truly international powerhouse in the airline world, but while it suited SIA for a while, it never grew into what it was hoped to be.

While Delta went from strength to strength — to the extent it is now regarded as one of the most profitable and successful of the US airlines — Swissair, on the other hand, effectively collapsed and its remnants with a complicated ownership structure was eventually taken over by Lufthansa in 2005.

Lufthansa and Air Canada entered into an agreement to work closely with SIA in 1998, two years before it became a fully-fledged member of the Star Alliance club.

In *Flying High in a Competitive Industry: Secrets of the World's Leading Airline*, the authors[1] write about alliances and in particular SIA's experience in such international partnerships.

SIA has been cautious in forging alliances, especially in its early days, operating a relatively small network of alliances.

They go on to say that alliances are "an important strategic option for airlines. Alliances that have attained the best results have typically brought together partners with complementary capabilities and compatible cultures as well as service levels".

Later, when Mr Lim was not on the airline board, SIA had some not so successful tie ups — its attempted take-over of Air New Zealand through the demise of Ansett in Australia was messy and costly.

SIA purchased 25% of Air New Zealand in 2000, however the airline came close to collapse, particularly after a mishandled alliance with Ansett in Australia, which in turn collapsed and the New Zealand government was left to rescue its airline. In the end, SIA's stake was reduced to 4.5% and this was subsequently sold in October 2004 at a substantial loss.

The acquisition of a large share of Virgin Atlantic which could have given SIA a foothold in the lucrative trans-Atlantic business, never delivered on its early promise.

It was of course after Mr Lim's time — and he is too polite to comment on what his successors did or didn't do right or wrong — SIA purchased a 49% stake in Virgin Atlantic Airways (Richard Branson's trans-Atlantic airline) in March 2000 for 600 million pounds. On December 2012, SIA sold its stake in Virgin for US$360 million, incurring a considerable loss.

Just like SIA shunned membership of IATA in its early years as it was seen as a restrictive industry body bent on stopping SIA from offering the "in-flight service that other airlines talk about", the airline did carefully consider a range of partnerships and agreements with other carriers.

Lim Chin Beng was ever patient, cautious and smart enough to know when to join and when to opt out.

Singapore Airlines did not go it alone for ever. After the agreeable split with Malaysia — when SIA and MAS were formed — it fought its own battles and won rights on merit.

Of course, there have been many mergers and acquisition and collapses in the airline business, as there has been in the automobile and other international industries.

It did not lose its interest in Virgin altogether though. In October 2012, it took a stake in Virgin Australia for A$105 million. This was strongly opposed by Qantas who saw this as a way international airlines — including Etihad and Air New Zealand, alongside SIA — would eat into their domestic business.

Karamjit Kaur wrote in *The Straits Times* (13 December 2013) that "SIA's ownership of Virgin Australia will go up from 19.8% to 21.2%"[2].

At the same time the report mentioned the airline was "strengthening its partnerships" with Taiwan's Eva Air, saying that "such partnerships were a key part of SIA's strategy to grow its network and reach without having to mount its own flights".

Besides their joint involvement in Virgin Australia and membership of the Star Alliance, SIA and Air New Zealand announced in 2014 a new "codeshare" partnership, with the New Zealand carrier returning to Singapore after eight years away with its own B777 services in January 2015[3].

While SIA always did have a subsidiary airline — Silk Air — it was never seen as a low cost or budget airline. It was more a regional shorter haul player, which SIA continues to own 100%. But in September 2004, maybe spurred on by the decision of its former boss to start Valueair, SIA took a 49% in Tiger, the rest belonging to Temasek Holdings and other investors.

When it was listed on the SGX in February 2011, Tiger showed that SIA shareholding was reduced to 34.4%. It has struggled to make a viable return, having a series of troubles in Australia and mixed blessings in Asia.

Again undeterred, SIA in 2012 invested in another start up low cost carrier Scoot, which announced itself to the world in November 2011. With aggressive advertising and a personable CEO — a former SIA man, Campbell Wilson, who originated in New Zealand — it is making waves, even if it is yet to make a profit.

While Mr Lim insists he does not regret what was done when he was in the hot seat, he also doesn't think it right to comment on the work and decisions of those who followed him. He admits he took risks, and — with the support of Mr Pillay and the board — made the bold decision in the airline's first year to opt for the bigger and costlier 747.

But the former airline boss does agree that joining the Star Alliance was a good move for SIA. A loose but helpful association of some of the world's leading airlines — and admittedly some they didn't see eye to eye with for some years in the 1970 and 1980s — are now sharing flights, services, code sharing — even sharing the same beds!

The Star Alliance network was established in 1997 as the first truly global airline alliance to offer worldwide reach, recognition and seamless service to the international traveller.

Its member airlines include some SIA has competed with vigorously at home and abroad — Lufthansa, Air Canada, Air New Zealand, and United. Some are certainly complementary and offer useful connections to bigger markets — like those from the African continent, Ethiopian Airlines and South African Airways.

Star Alliance's acceptance by the market has been recognised by numerous awards — something to add to SIA's own healthy collection — including the Air Transport World Market Leadership Award and Best Airline Alliance by both Business Traveller Magazine and Skytrax.

Overall, the Star Alliance network offers (in mid-2014) more than 18,000 daily flights to 1,269 airports in 193 countries.

One of the big advantages, for the traveller at least, is that alliance members aim to provide the nearest thing to seamless travel with connecting flights at the same airport.

In June 2014, Her Majesty Queen Elizabeth II formally opened the new home of Star Alliance at London's Heathrow Airport, unveiling a plaque that names the facility "Terminal 2: The Queen's Terminal", in recognition of her long association with the airport[4].

This latest addition to Heathrow airport, according to media reports, will house all 23 Star Alliance member airlines that serve the UK's only hub airport. So far, United, Air Canada, Air China and ANA have successfully commenced operations there and the remaining airlines will move in gradually by November 2014. This schedule ensures each move is as smooth as possible for passengers.

Observing what other airlines do, inside or outside alliances, Mr Lim notices that the Middle East carriers — Etihad, Emirates and Qatar — are doing things very similar to what SIA did in its earlier days. Expanding rapidly, offering cheaper fares to build market share and investing heavily — even more than SIA did — in aircraft, in flight service, international pilots, and cabin crew, advertising, and sponsorships around the world. The name Etihad, for example, appears on a number of sports stadiums.

Also — unlike SIA — the Middle East carriers have relied on a big supply of soft loans and willing donors. They have also started to take on the mantle of SIA where in-flight service and reliability goes. Now you will more than likely see at least one of the Middle East carriers — Emirates for example — among the top ten airlines.

SIA has maintained it reputation for service and through its wise choice of partners and its clever advertising has maintained a high business profile and remained economically viable. It's tough, as Mr Lim acknowledges, when airlines, like media companies, tourist organisations and property businesses, feel the full brunt of financial crises, global or regional health scares — like the devastating SARS virus — terrorism and all the other man-made or natural disasters, wars, volcanic eruptions, fuel hikes and environmental impacts.

The last twenty years has seen them all impact airlines and international travel. So going it alone — in the face of all the added impacts around — is harder than ever. Being in the same club as others can help cushion the impact of outside events. Shared resources and shared risks. Like belonging to a health insurance plan.

Reflecting on airline industry practices past and present, Mr Lim was always keen to explore opportunities for collaboration and partnerships. Without infringing on the rules of competition and free trade, he sees that much can be gained by industry players working together.

There is also much more unity among airlines now — united for success — and IATA is playing a much more positive role, as even Mr Lim acknowledges.

In tough times — as many of the world's full-service airlines are experiencing currently — it helps to have partners to turn to and work with. But like any partnership — marriage as well — there is a responsibility on members to give and take. And a weakness in one partner can impact on the other.

Mr Lim would have to agree with the *Financial Times'* Andrew Hill — quoted at the start of this chapter — that "business partnerships would be more durable if the joys of the partnering part were offset more frequently by the realities of the business bit".

Endnotes

1. From *Flying High in a Competitive Industry: Secrets of the World's Leading* Airline by Louis Heracleous, Jochen Wirtz and Nitin Pangarkar (McGraw Hill, 2009).

2. "SIA expanding reach with airline tie-ups" by Karamjit Kaur (13 December 2013), *The Straits Times*.

3. Reported in *International Business Times* on 26 September 2014 announcing Air New Zealand's return to Singapore and its new codeshare partnership with SIA.

4. Press Release on HRM Queen Elizabeth II's plaque and on Star Alliance feature at Heathrow and is available at http://www.staralliance.com/en/press/queen-opens-lhr-t2-prp/.

Miss Singapore in Future: Costumed young Singapore girls decorate the cover for Miss Universe Pageant 1987 programme and appeared on stage as well, when Lim Chin Beng, as the Tourist Board Chairman, made sure the event was well hosted and attracted international media attention for Singapore. (From the programme produced by Singapore Tourism Board and in the Lim family collection.)

"On a little street in Singapore
With me — beside a lotus covered door
A veil of moonlight on her lovely face
How pale the hands that held me in embrace".

(The song made famous by the Manhatten Transfer,
"On a Little Street in Singapore",
written by Peter De Rose/Billy Hill in the 1930s.)

CHAPTER 21

EVENTFUL TIMES

I f there is one event to stand out during Lim Chin Beng's reign as Chairman of the Singapore Tourism Board it would be the Miss Universe Pageant in 1987.

For the record, Wikipedia memorably recounts the event this way:

> *Miss Universe 1987, the 36th Miss Universe Pageant was held at Hall Four at World Trade Centre, Singapore on 27 May 1987. 22-year-old Cecilia Bolocco of Chile was crowned as Miss Universe 1987 by the outgoing titleholder, Barbara Palacios Teyde of Venezuela. 68 contestants competed in the 1987 Miss Universe Pageant. This was the twenty-first and final Miss Universe competition to be hosted by popular American television host Bob Barker.*

But for Mr Lim and the STB staff, supporters and the total tourism, hotel and events industry of Singapore there was much more to it than that.

There was much behind the scenes and on stage that kept everyone associated with it well and truly occupied. From day one — four weeks before the event was televised — when the attractive young ladies first started arriving into Singapore, there was an accompanying stream of minders, organisers, technical and creative people and the television team from CBS and Paramount, who owned the show.

While the event itself would not only be screened throughout the United States — great market for Singapore — but coverage was also picked up by TV channels in more than 50 other countries.

As there were 68 entrants present in Singapore, other media took a lot of interest in the event. Fuelled by the Singapore-based PR team, media based in Singapore and journalists visiting for the occasion, would be sending more stories and photographs of the contestants every day for a month from Singapore. Often capturing a pretty and young "ambassador" for one of the 68 countries in a suitable Singapore location — the famed Singapore Zoo, Chinatown, Botanic Gardens or Sentosa Island.

The Singapore based media — foreign and local — seemingly could not get enough of the event's stars. Every day, during the month, one of the international news agencies based in the city state, noted that they were providing overseas media with an average of seven photographs a day on Miss Universe contestants and related events. In a normal month — which May 1987 certainly was not — the agency would usually despatch no more than five photographs. For the whole month!

The tourist board made sure all locations where used at some stage for visits by the girls as well as to include in filming of different segments for the final TV show.

The three new hotels in the Marina Square had just opened — Mandarin Oriental, Marina Mandarin and Pan Pacific — and they became not only home for the contestants for the best part of a month, but headquarters for a lot of the activity around the event.

Even a quaint song "On a Little Street in Singapore", made famous by Manhattan Transfer, was included in the big opening number to get the TV show underway, accompanied by images of the girls in Singapore street locations.

Mr Lim will admit that much of what went on during that action-filled month in 1987 is something of a blur these days, but he is sure he met each one of the visiting beauties at some stage and he was on hand at all the official engagements, including the big night.

He also contributed a very notable message into the official programme, which drew attention to the importance of the event for Singapore[1]:

> *An international Pageant like this also adds colour and excitement to Singapore — for our own people and for our visitors. It perhaps typifies what tourism can do for a relatively small nation. It puts us in touch with the world; it broadens our experience of other countries and people; and it entertains and enlightens us all.*
>
> *The Pageant is being held at a particularly fortuitous time. Singapore has embarked on a major plan to preserve its character and charm, to revitalise and upgrade our existing attractions, as well as develop new ones. All this will go towards making Singapore an even more appealing island for our own people as well as our very welcome visitors.*

He and others at the Board also made sure Singapore got to meet the stars of the show. There was little obvious security and the girls had some free time to engage in the twin Singaporean passions, shopping and eating out. Singaporeans were also called on to volunteer for "duties" — each girl had a locally-appointed chaperone for example — and there was no shortage of people willing to get involved.

Besides the big show at the World Trade Centre — televised and shown locally for all to enjoy — there was one other impromptu event that really brought the Miss Universe event and contestants home to Singapore. It was arranged for a number of vintage and classic cars to transport the girls — two in a car — down Orchard Road.

While police approval was given to the "drive-by", no-one could have predicted the attention it would attract. It literally stopped the traffic in Orchard Road, as swarms of people got as close to the cars and "stars" as possible. Board officers, PR people and volunteers did their best to keep the cars moving without anyone getting in the way, but it was for Singapore such a spontaneous outpouring of enthusiasm, usually reserved for famous celebrities.

Mr Lim was impressed then, as he is now when he recalls the way all of Singapore pulled together to make it an event to remember and which had such impact at home and abroad.

He noted this in his Miss Universe Pageant message, by saying:

> *In planning attractions and facilities for tourists, as well as host-*
> *ing events like this Miss Universe Pageant, the Singapore Tourist*
> *Promotion Board is always mindful of what is also good for*
> *Singaporeans.*
>
> *Singapore's support and interest in this Pageant convinces us that*
> *we are on the right track. Singaporeans want to see more major*
> *international events, whether they be sporting, artistic or enter-*
> *taining in nature. The enthusiasm that has greeted Singapore's*
> *commitment to preserve and develop our historic and culturally*
> *significant attractions tells us that these projects are seen as a*
> *move to enrich the lives of Singaporeans as well as add to*
> *Singapore's appeal as a destination for tourists.*

Of course there was generous sponsorship. From Singapore Airlines for one, which reportedly provided around S$1 million worth of travel, and from the hotels and transport suppliers who contributed willingly to make it a stand-out event.

It was also a critical part of the plan, which Mr Lim and other Board members and staff had committed to, to spend money and a lot of effort to put Singapore on the global map. It worked for the month and it worked for many months after.

Staging and attracting events like Miss Universe was also a key part of the Tourism Product Development Plan launched in 1986. The S$1 billion plan aimed to increase visitor arrivals, length of stay and tourist expenditure. Besides greater international advertising and media exposure, it also outlined action plans for the restoration and revitalisation of older areas such as Chinatown and Little India, the greening of the whole island and the cleaning up of the Singapore River.

It was a conscious decision to make sure these attractions were drawn into the Miss Universe Pageant, through strategic visits by the girls as well as filmed inserts for the television production.

The plan was quite specific in that it created five major themes (exotic east, colonial heritage, tropical island resort, clean and green garden city, and centre for international sporting events), each of which was expected to generate half-day or day-long visits by tourists.

Miss Universe, according to Mr Lim, played an important part in highlighting all that was memorable and attractive about a visit. And the girls added glamour as well.

The special report in the *Media and Marketing* magazine at the time (3 July 1997) notes rather excitedly[2]:

> *The winner of the 1987 Miss Universe pageant is Miss Chile Cecilia Bolocco. Of course, everybody knows that. But perhaps the real winner was Singapore, as the S$6.5 million (about US$3 million) host of the media extravaganza.*
>
> *With the hosting of the event which attracted an estimated worldwide audience of 600 million viewers in 54 countries, the spotlight was turned full-blast on Singapore. On top of that was the press coverage given to the 68 entrants leading up to the finals and the winner.*

But for the Tourism Board and its Chairman, Singapore did not intend to be likened to a pop star as a "one-hit wonder". Great as the Miss Universe was, it was seen as part of a continuing process to stage and attract events with class and impact. To draw attention to the city's cultural heritage and its more modern attractions.

There followed a series of events — in the arts and sports — during Mr Lim's time. The Singapore Arts Festival was promoted widely overseas — not just to draw international acts, but for visiting media and audiences to come and enjoy as well.

Getting media to focus on Singapore had not been a problem but in the mid-1980s it was starting to get greater competition from other places.

So international PR was stepped up and many more journalists were invited — often jointly arranged with SIA and the Tourism Board — to enjoy the events, the food, and the attractions such a multi-cultural place offered.

In the same *Media and Marketing* magazine article, it noted that in the month after the Miss Universe Pageant which had acted as such a strong media draw, Singapore had a visit by the popular television programme *Runaway with the Rich and Famous*, an Australian fashion magazine doing a fashion shoot in Singapore and other visiting journalists from Australia, the UK, Germany and the USA.

Often Mr Lim was called on to meet and be interviewed by visiting journalists and also be pictured attending important events.

Never one to bathe in reflected glory, never-the-less the "quite achiever" for Singapore tourism, was not only helping to attract major events to Singapore — often pulling off joint "deals" because of his unique SIA/STB roles — he was also making sure the world knew what Singapore was about.

Lim Chin Beng was a "man with a mission" — to launch Singapore tourism into new heights — and Miss Universe, with its glamour, international appeal and media impact, proved to be an ideal launch pad.

Endnotes

1. Mr Lim's message in the official programme for the Miss Universe Pageant, 1987.
2. A copy of the 3 July 1987 edition of *Media and Marketing* which had a "special report" on the Miss Universe pageant in Singapore is in the author's possession, as he is quoted in the report and he also drew on this report for other information in this chapter.

Proper Place: The Ascott serviced apartments, located in the old Asia Insurance Building, one of the few historic structures which have retained a place for people in the commercial heart of Singapore. (An Ascott Group/CapitaLand photo.)

"Property is intended to serve life, and no matter how much we surround it with rights and respect, it has no personal being. It is part of the earth man walks on. It is not man".

(Martin Luther King, Jr., *The Trumpet of Conscience*, 1967)

CHAPTER 22

PROPERTY GURU

One would not normally associate the acquisition or sale of property to this thoroughly-entrenched airline man. But the property industry was quick to knock on Lim Chin Beng's door and ask him to do for property what he had excelled at in airlines and tourism.

So when the paint was hardly dry on the completion of his airline directorship and diplomat service, he was whisked into the board rooms of some of the biggest property players in Singapore.

While he is quick to insist that he did not have any serious interest in the property business, he cannot dispute the fact that he was an independent board director — and in some cases chairman as well — of a number of large property companies. Between 1998 and 2012 he served as a director of at least 20 companies — and six as chairman of the board — and more than half of them had property as a primary focus.

It all started in 1998, when he became a director of Pontiac Land — which included its Ritz Carlton Millennia hotel and property businesses — and Pidemco, which morphed into CapitaLand in 2000 along with another clutch of property responsibilities. And he stayed with both for more than ten years. Around the same time, CapitaLand was coming into its own, two of the companies it inherited were also merged. Somerset Holdings, with Mr Lim in the chair, joined forces with The Ascott Limited to become The

Ascott Group, producing in the process the Asia Pacific's largest serviced residence company, with assets of S$2.7 billion[1].

A word from the merged entity's Chairman in the press announcement at the time (16 October 2000):

> *With the successful merger, our vision now spans beyond the Asia Pacific to Europe and the US. As market leaders in the Asia Pacific, we already have significant presence and brand equity in most of the countries we operate in. This is an excellent platform from which to compete for international leadership and establish global brands.*

Then the Group had a portfolio of 6,000 residence units in 16 cities in 10 countries, spanning from Auckland, New Zealand to London in the United Kingdom. It also had as its flagship property the very distinctive and historic former Asia Insurance Building, located on Finlayson Green near Raffles Place, in Singapore's downtown[2].

On 4 July 2006, Mr Lim was the one to announce that Group's purchase of the important property:

> *In recent years, the supply of high-end, good quality accommodation in Singapore has been reduced as the number of four and five-star hotels have been converted into condominiums. With the government's efforts to attract more visitors to Singapore, the proposed acquisitions of Asia Insurance Building and Hotel Asia by Ascott will be timely to cater to the expected increase in demand for good quality accommodation for extended stay.*

He stayed in the Ascott Chairman's role for 12 years, enjoying the international flavour of the business which went beyond property to cater for the business traveller and the service industry, which also drew on his tourism industry and promotion experience.

A year after that notable purchase, Mr Lim was to introduce some senior management changes which saw someone who had worked with him at the Tourist Board some years previously, come on board.

Jennie Chua — who had formerly been also General Manager of Raffles Hotel — became the group's President and Chief Executive Officer. She saw the opportunity to "drive for greater growth and achieve our global expansion objectives by capitalising on our pole position in the serviced residence industry"[3].

But the Ascott Group was just "one of the strings to his bow". This multi-talented former double bass player seemed to be taking on even more director roles, resembling more a conductor and orchestra leader at the same time. And property and tourism tunes seemed to be recurring ones.

For property and tourism came together with Mr Lim's involvement as a director of Pontiac Land, which also included being a director of four related businesses — Pontiac Hotels, Pontiac Land, Ritz Carlton Millennia Hotels and RCMS Properties.

During his four years as Chairman of Singapore Press Holdings, property was definitely in the media and management mix there as well, as the annual report of 2005 noted[4]:

> *Revenue from our property segment went up 8.3% to [S]$89.4 million. We expect the amalgamated Paragon, which enjoys 100% occupancy in its retail space, to continue to yield more than 10% return on equity per annum. Other property assets, including the Times Industrial Building site, will be divested at the appropriate time to maximise shareholder value.*

Another very important property in the SPH portfolio, which had more than sentimental value for all the journalists and editors who had been based there over the years, was the landmark Times House. In 2003, the SPH Board approved the sale of Times House to Marco Polo Developments for S$118.88 million.

The National Archives records this historical move this way[5]:

> *Times House, a building that once stood at the junction of Kim Seng Road and River Valley Road, was officially opened on 3 April 1958. Forty-six years later, on 1 April 2004, it got its first taste of the cruncher that targets to demolish the building in four months. The news-making occupants of Times House had moved*

*to the new News Centre in Toa Payoh North two years earlier,
leaving behind memories of a building that was the hotbed of news
in Singapore for over four decades. A new condominium will rise
on the site of the demolished building.*

Two of Singapore's Presidents Wee Kim Wee and SR Nathan had worked out of Times House and both had connections with Lim Chin Beng.

Mr Wee joined *The Straits Times* family in 1930 as a clerk before becoming a reporter focusing on political issues. He eventually became one of the paper's main reporters. After a few years working for wire agencies he returned to *The Straits Times* in 1959 and was appointed deputy editor in Singapore. Like Mr Lim, he also studied at Raffles Institution, albeit a few years earlier, and also preceded Mr Lim as Singapore Ambassador to Japan. Mr Wee also served as a diplomat in South Korea and Malaysia. He served as President from 2 September 1985 to 1 September 1993[6].

SR Nathan was the Chairman of SPH from 1982 to 1988 and went on to be Singapore's first elected President, the position he held for two terms, from September 1999 to September 2011.

Besides the SPH chairmanship, Messrs Nathan and Lim had another property connection in common.

Mr Nathan, after his service as Singapore's President, became Chairman of Capital Land Hope Foundation, a role Mr Lim had played previously.

As a Director of CapitaLand for all those years — 1998 to 2010 — Mr Lim also had the responsibility for its charitable arm for seven years until 2012, when Mr Nathan stepped in.

Familiar with the workings of Foundations, as he had also served as a director of the Press Foundation of Singapore (which later changed its name to Singapore Press Holdings Foundation), Mr Lim enjoyed his time identifying with those less fortunate at home and aboard and seeing that worthwhile educational projects were funded.

A good example of this was when CapitaLand and Singapore's five Community Development Councils announced in 20 April 2011 that its Green for Hope programme was extending its reach to beneficiaries island-wide[7].

As Chairman of CapitaLand Hope Foundation, Mr Lim said at the time said:

> *The Green for Hope campaign is in line with the Foundation's focus on supporting programmes for the shelter, education and healthcare needs of underprivileged children. Since the campaign's launch, over 2400 tonnes of paper, plastic and aluminium have been recycled through the green efforts of CapitaLand's tenants, shoppers and serviced residence guests, as well as primary schools across Singapore.*
>
> *CapitaLand Hope Foundation's total donation of over S$3.2 million since 2008 has benefited underprivileged children from 10 children's charities and 170 primary schools. We are pleased to partner all five Community Development Councils for the first time in Green for Hope @ CapitaLand 2011, extending our donations to a wider community and reaching more beneficiaries across Singapore.*

CapitaLand, and its charitable arm, went beyond Singapore, and once again Mr Lim enjoyed being involved with an organization which had such an international focus.

When he was one of its directors, CapitaLand was recognised as one of Asia's largest real estate companies. Its real estate and hospitality portfolio, which includes homes, offices, shopping malls, serviced residences and mixed developments, spans more than 110 cities in over 20 countries.

CapitaLand Hope Foundation was established in 2005 to further the property company's corporate commitment to build a better future for underprivileged children. Its focus was to support programmes for the shelter, education and healthcare needs of underprivileged children in Singapore and overseas.

The people factor was always important to Mr Lim, perhaps even more than a massive property portfolio.

It was the people who knew him who invited him onto the boards in the first place and the people he worked with whom he cared about. That kept him keen, motivated and committed.

He said as much when he completed his tenure at SPH in 2005 and in his special message noted that despite the best efforts of the Board, through a difficult period, some jobs were lost and this would always weigh on their hearts and minds. "For this I must thank our staff — our most valuable asset — who hunkered down and persevered through the trying times".

Being a man who cared about people was undoubtedly on his mind when he took on the directorship at Starhub in 1998 — even before the upstart telecoms player in Singapore started its business in 2000 to challenge the status quo and the long established Singapore Telecoms. It was people more than property which occupied his time and attention.

In his 12 years on the board at Starhub, he admits he was particularly interested in human resource areas. He might have been new to telecommunications but he knew a lot about managing a people business and treating people as a valued asset.

At the same time he relished being part of a new enterprise in the business of competing against an entrenched player. That reminded him somewhat of the role he played in the early days at SIA as a new entrant competing against the big boys of the established international airlines.

He also relished being part of an organisation committed to doing good — for its own people and the community at large. He could identify with the corporate social responsibility commitment made by Starhub to conduct business in a sustainable manner: "we continuously strive for a harmonious balance between our economic, social and environmental objectives"[8].

Being a business leader who strongly believes in transparency and fairness, he also agreed wholeheartedly with Starhub's ethos which is still "constantly guided by Ethics, Corporate Governance, Human Rights, Environmental Responsibility and Civic Mindedness".

Just like StarHub is still committed to "making a difference in the world in which we live", that could well be the unwritten driving force in the life and times of Lim Chin Beng, whether in property, airlines, tourism, aerospace industries or events.

Whether sitting at the head of a distinguished board room table or in negotiation mode with Japanese bureaucrats, whether on the shop floor or the press room, in the aircraft hangar or the building site, in his conducive

Airline House office or travelling in the comfort of an airline seat 35,000 feet above land, this man of the people always had his feet on the ground.

He knew how to lead, but it never required him to thump the table. He influenced and he guided discussion. He always sought consensus and always listened to all viewpoints. But at the same time this "quiet achiever" was a tough negotiator. But the art of negotiation — and company leadership — was to enable others to feel that they achieved what they wanted and they were part of the right decision. He would have to agree with the tongue in cheek observation of the British television presenter and interviewer David Frost who said "diplomacy is the art of letting somebody else have your way"!

He applied that to his board roles and to his dealing with all people, even seemingly intransigent union officials, who would leave his office "happy" even though he had done little more than listen, nod and smile. He was a good listener and his door was always open.

He was firm in his belief in fairness and doing good. People were the "most valuable asset" wherever he was around.

He also points out that he was his own man. In spite of his early work as a civil servant, managing the national carrier, representing the country as a diplomat, serving on Singapore's Public Service Commission and the Legal Service Commission — both for ten years — he was independent to the core.

Even at SPH, where the board had such a "pedigree" of senior civil servants and cabinet ministers as its chairmen and directors, he insists he was "apo-litical". He was not a politician or a member of a political party. He was neutral, independent and proudly so.

While he would never deny the importance of profitability for all of the businesses he was involved with over his 52 working years — from the time he started with Malayan Airways in 1960 until his retirement from all board positions in 2012 — it was the people factor which kept rising to the top.

He has shown by example that by focussing on people — the customer and the employee — you can achieve so much more. Profit as well!

From setting the scene for SIA which looked after its customers better than anyone else — "in-flight service even other airlines talk about" — to rec-ognising that employees are a company's "most valuable asset", Mr Lim has showed time and time again that managing a company for people can also be a profitable business.

So maybe the words of Martin Luther King are as relevant today as ever, even though they might at first seem to be out of place for a "property guru" or anyone in big business today.

"Property is intended to serve life".

But it is true, in the same way that the property companies Lim Chin Beng has been associated with over the years all showed that they can serve the needs of the people and the community in more ways than one.

Property is all about putting people in their rightful place.

Endnotes

1. Ascott and Somerset merger announcement. Available at http://www.theascottlimited. com/en/investorinfo/news/news459.html.

2. Ascott Group's News release on the acquisition of Asia Insurance Building is available at http://www.theascottlimited.com/en/investorinfo/news/news692.html.

3. Ascott Group's announcement on management changes is available at http://www.theas-cottlimited.com/en/investorinfo/news/news737.html.

4. Singapore Press Holding 2005 Annual Report is available at http://sph.listedcompany. com/misc/sph_ar2005.pdf.

5. On the demise of Times House, see http://eresources.nlb.gov.sg/infopedia/articles/ SIP_581_2005-01-19.html.

6. Biographical information on Wee Kim Wee is available at http://www.istana.gov.sg/content/ istana/thepresident/formerpresidents/wkw.html.

7. News release on CapitaLand Hope Foundation and its Green for Hope programme (20 April 2011), is available at http://media.corporate-ir.net/Media_Files/IROL/13/130462/ announcements/2011announcements/April/NewsRelease.GFH2011.FINAL.pdf.

8. Starhub's Corporate Sustainability and Responsibility can be found at http://www.starhub. com/about-us/corporate-sustainability-and-responsibility.html.

Back to the Future: Lim Chin Beng forecasts that supersonic commercial aircraft like this will return to the skies, albeit quieter and larger to accommodate more passengers than the Concorde, seen here in the days when it regularly flew into Paya Lebar Airport in SIA colours in the 1970s. (From the Singapore Airlines collection.)

"For once you have tasted flight you will walk the earth with your eyes turned skywards, for there you have been and there you will long to return".

(Leonardo da Vinci, 1452–1519)

CHAPTER 23

FLYING INTO THE FUTURE

I s the future of flight something dreams are made of or is it much more down to earth?

Do we aspire to quietly fly with the angels or the birds? Or blast off into space at the unbearable speed of light to break the sound barrier? Or do we just want to enjoy the air travel experience as much as we welcome arriving at our destination?

Airbus conducted a very comprehensive survey in 2012 involving 10,000 people around the world who said what they wanted from the future of flight. The call was definitely for more flying, in a more sustainable way and a less stressful experience. Here are a few of the key findings:

- 63% of people worldwide say they will fly more by 2050
- 60% do not think social media will replace the need to see people face-to-face
- 96% believe aircraft will need to be more sustainable or 'eco-efficient'
- Almost 40% feel air travel (door-to-door) is increasingly stressful
- 86% of people think less fuel burn is key
- 85% want to see a reduction in carbon emissions
- 66% want quieter aircraft
- 65% would like to see planes which are fully recyclable.

Besides carrying out such an educational survey, Airbus is doing a lot of work on design for future flight, including creating radical blueprints for concept planes and aircraft interiors. It is all about learning more of the technologies and innovations that come together in an engineer's dream for a concept plane. It is also using 'biomimicry' or biologically inspired engineering. A growing number of aeronautical innovations are inspired by an array of natural structures, organs and materials. These tried and tested patterns of the natural world will continue to be a powerful source of inspiration in the future[1].

Lim Chin Beng is an airline man who has lived through practically all stages of the development of flight — through nine of the eleven decades since the first commercial flight got off the ground in 1914 — so not only does he know a thing or two about the past and present flying machines, but he has some perceptive views for the future too.

With or without family, he has travelled, seen the sights and experienced the delays and difficulties all travellers encounter.

But he has maintained his love of travel, his love for nature, his love for meeting and enjoying the company of people and places.

When he last visited Japan (in 2013) he was sorry that he just missed the cherry blossom time because he knows how beautiful and memorable such an encounter with nature is.

On a recent visit to the United States (in 2014), he missed getting to the famed Yellowstone National Park — where he had always wanted to go — as it is where nature and man struggle to maintain equilibrium but where conservation currently succeeds in a place bursting with untapped geothermal energy.

And while he loves his home and country and all they offer, he cannot stop wanting to travel, to explore, to go to places familiar and places off the beaten track.

While his personal mobility is not what it used to be, air travel still enables him to go far from home and experience what he says everyone should enjoy — the exhilaration, the pleasure, the peacefulness — of far-away places, meeting people and learning about other cultures.

When Mr Lim talked about tourism and its benefits to a conference in Singapore way back in 1988, he pointed to the five important factors for the tourist industry to always bear in mind: the economic and the manpower factors for a start, which were so important for the economic viability and sustainability of the industry (see Chapter 18).

He put equal emphasis on what matters to people, to the tourists themselves. He points to the cultural factor and the exotic factor. Being conscious of the cultural and social implications as well as impacts of tourism — whether intended or not — as well as providing for the human craving for exoticism and excitement.

But the fifth factor, which was very relevant to him at the time when he was both an airline man and a committed promoter of a tourist destination (Singapore), was the accessibility factor.

He called for the industry — airlines, civil aviation authorities and tourism organisations — "to bring down the barriers to travel".

Has that happened in the 26 years since he articulated that so well?

Certainly he sees that practically everyone can travel overseas now. It is cheaper with the low cost carriers making overseas travel often as cheap as a train journey or bus tour.

He also sees that countries which once restricted the overseas travel of its own people have brought down those barriers. To such an extent that China — as the one country which had the most outbound travel rules — now contributes more tourists than any other country to most places in the world.

The UN World Tourism Organisation noted in January 2014 that "China, which became the largest outbound market in 2012 with an expenditure of US$102 billion, saw an increase in expenditure of 28% in the first three quarters of 2013"[2].

In 2013, the number of outbound tourists from China totalled 98.19 million, up 18% compared with 2012. At present, China has increased the number of permitted overseas destinations for its citizens to 150 countries and regions[3].

So are all the barriers removed?

Not quite, says Mr Lim, the visionary and close observer of airline and travel trends for the past 50-odd years.

Freedom of the skies is still not a reality everywhere. Great strides have been made and most of the worst protectionist countries have opened up and allowed airlines of other countries access to destinations and markets.

He would like to see more being done in the future to make sure there are no barriers to airlines or the countries they originate from or want to fly to and through.

The flying experience has certainly improved with newer and more efficient aircraft, but as more are flying and the low cost carriers have helped make that happen, the infrastructure on the ground has struggled to keep up.

He believes the pleasure of travel — now and in the future — should start with the airport experience. He is well aware that some airports are bad enough to put people off air travel for life!

Some airports are managing very well because they plan ahead. At Singapore Changi Airport, the comfort and convenience of the passenger is uppermost and it still wins awards, he is pleased to see, because management is thinking ahead and providing for the future of air travel now.

How does Changi do it? While always making sure security and safety is taken into account, there is remarkably good co-operation amongst all the Government agencies — immigration, customs, police — to ensure that departures and arrivals go smoothly. Good systems are in place to cope with the growing volume of traffic day and night.

An example, not only as to how Singapore thinks ahead, but also to show how willing it is to share, is the planned World Airport Expo in February 2015[4].

It is an event with the future very much in mind. But practical too. It is endorsed by Changi Airport Group (CAG) and Civil Aviation Authority of Singapore (CAAS), stakeholders of the world's most awarded airport.

Singapore is never resting on its laurels. Mr Lim knows for a fact. It is gearing up for an even bigger and brighter future. It offers one of the most ambitious airport and terminal development plan anywhere in the world. By the early 2020s, Singapore expects to complete an entirely new Terminal 4 and hopes to have ready what is expected to be one of the world's largest airport terminals, the all new Terminal 5. By then Changi will also have a third runway operational.

Ramping up the ability to cater for more and more travellers and shippers of goods in the future is what more countries and cities need to be able to do.

So besides people transport, airlines must also do a better job of facilitating the shipping of goods around the world.

SIA, for one, has long held on to the belief that freight is of great economic importance, to the extent that in July 1992, a fully-fledged cargo division was formed to devote even more attention to the cargo business. As a further step in its evolution, it formed itself into an independently managed sub-sidiary of Singapore Airlines on the 1st July 2001.

Singapore Airlines Cargo (SIA Cargo) now offers more than 900 flights a week from its Singapore hub, linking more than 70 cities in over 35 countries across 6 continents with its fleet of dedicated B747-400 freighters, as well as belly capacities of passenger aircraft operated by Singapore Airlines[5].

When the Lim Chin Beng and son Arthur started Valuair in 2004 they were determined to do what other budget airlines didn't do and that was to provide space for cargo as well as passengers.

It is of note that the new Singapore start-up Scoot — which appears to be modelled more on Valuair than any other budget carrier — provides some "frills" along with lower fares. It also caters for cargo shippers, working closely with SIA Cargo.

The intrusion of drones — unmanned aircraft used largely up until now for military purposes — into the preserve of air freight companies for ship-ment of goods and mail deliveries, should make some airlines sit up to see what the flying freight future holds. Reuters reports that Google and Amazon are trialing drones for deliveries[6]: "Google is developing airborne drones capable of flying on their own and delivering anything from candy to medi-cine. The effort, which Google calls Project Wing, marks the company's latest expansion beyond its Web-based origins and could help Google break into lucrative markets such as commerce and package delivery, ratcheting up the competition with Amazon.com".

Reuters reported that Google rival Amazon.com announced plans last year (2013) to use aerial delivery drones for a service called "Prime Air".

In 2012, the United States Congress required the Federal Aviation Administration (FAA) to establish a road map for the broader use of drones.

The FAA has allowed limited use of drones in the US for surveillance, law enforcement, atmospheric research and other applications, Reuters reports.

New York Times reported on 25 September 2014 that DHL owned by Deutsche Post, has trialled the use of drones for freight deliveries in Germany[7].

So for the future and for now, a passenger, like the freight shipper, must have a genuine choice.

There needs to be three passenger travel choices, according to Mr Lim, which airlines have tried for some time to fit into the same aircraft. But now airlines can be differentiated by what they offer. The low, cheaper genuine budget carrier, for one, is the entry level as it helps more people get to where they want to go at some unbelievably low prices.

Then there must be the airlines that offer a certain level of comfort and convenience, in the medium price range. That's what Valueair set out to do and there are others doing that. Air Asia — while it is still regarded as a budget carrier — is offering such a range of frequent scheduled services that it is meeting the needs of the mid-level air traveller. As is Scoot in Asia and Virgin in Australia.

And then there's the higher cost and class of service which business travellers are prepared to pay more for. The trouble is some airlines have been so reliant on this traffic and they are all competing for the same business. Some are "going for broke" in the process.

Instead of having the one airline offering three classes on the same aircraft, Mr Lim sees the trend towards differentiation — one airline offering one class of travel. And a choice for the passenger based on service, comfort, convenience and cost.

He told MBA students in 2005[8]:

> I would venture that the sector length of future flights will be determined not by the technical aspect of the aircraft but by the maximum hours that passengers can endure being cooped up in an aircraft. Another interesting aviation milestone is that all the world's B747s have flown a total distance equivalent to 75000 round trips from earth to the moon!

Talking about the moon, what about space travel?

He is well aware of the plans of Sir Richard Branson and other transport entrepreneurs like Elon Musk to take passengers into space and bring them back.

A report in the UK's *Daily Mail* in 29 May 2014 confirmed that Richard Branson's dream to charter commercial space flights has taken a step closer to reality. The report said his company, Virgin Galactic, "signed a deal with US aviation authorities to let it blast paying customers into space. Commercial flights are to begin by the end of this year and more than 600 people have already signed up at US$250,000 each to take a trip on SpaceShipTwo"[9].

The innovative and inventive Elon Musk, who is already making waves with his powerful electric car, the Tesla and with a solar energy company Solar City, attracts as much praise as he does doubts about his space attempts, as this Guardian report by Joe Pappalardo on 26 June this year indicates[10]:

"Musk — the insanely dedicated, wealthy and polarizing founder of PayPal, Tesla and Space Exploration Technologies (SpaceX) — is on a hot streak when it comes to spaceflight. He's raiding revenue streams from NASA and the US military to fund a private manned space program. His main weapon: low prices, with SpaceX offering satellite launches at about one-fifth the price of competitors at just over $60m a pop".

Pappalardo also noted that not having the volume to cater for the masses will make it expensive. "But perhaps it can be likened to the early days of flight — when only the very wealthy went on the early continent/ocean crossing journeys on flying boats…Clipper and Shorts Imperial".

A third space flight option is currently on offer to would-be amateur astronauts and even Singaporeans were being targeted at a special promotion in August this year (2014), according to this Channel News Asia report:[11]

> *Flying into space is now within reach for Singaporeans who wish to do so — but the experience comes at a hefty price of S$100,000 for a ticket.*

The report continued, that for that amount, passengers can experience a space shuttle takeoff and a view of the Earth. The total flight time will take about one hour including takeoff and landing. "As the shuttle has only two seats, passengers get to play the role of a co-pilot, performing tasks such as navigation".

The news report pointed out there was a prerequisite though — passengers need to be certified fit by a doctor. After that, the passenger will have to undergo a compulsory training programme in the Netherlands.

US-based XCOR Space Expeditions, which develops commercial space shuttles, launched the sale of tickets in Singapore in partnership with Luminox watches.

It is scheduled to make its first worldwide launch into space, from its spaceport in Curacao, an island in the southern Caribbean Sea, by the end of 2015.

Mr Lim would not be the only one to question whether space travel can become within the reach of enough people to make it viable, but he does agree that aviation has made great strides since the early island-hopping days and nights of international air travel in flying boats from the 1930s to the 1950s, which were definitely reserved for the very rich.

Maybe one day in the future — thanks to the pioneering work of Virgin Galactic, SpaceX and XCOR, along with their NASA predecessors — space flight will be safe and value for money. But Mr Lim thinks that is a long way ahead.

What is more realistic and more achievable is a return to supersonic travel. He predicted its return when he spoke to the MBA students in 2005[12]:

> *Looking further into the future, I am convinced that the supersonic airplane will make a comeback. With an ideal size of say 300 seats, the range capability to fly across the Pacific, quieter and more efficient engines and capable of flying at a speed of Mach 3, it should prove very popular with the businessmen. The second generation SST would allow businessmen to have face to face meetings without having to waste too much time travelling long distances and spending long periods away from their offices.*
>
> *Some airports may specialise in handling the SST, some in handling the ultra long haul flights and become major aviation hubs.*

Some may even specialise in handling budget airlines. But what is certain is that airports that do not change, coupled with an aviation policy that is restrictive, will degenerate into insignificant airports catering to perhaps just domestic flights and a few international flights, instead of becoming important international aviation hubs.

It wasn't just the Concorde disaster on take-off at Charles de Gaulle Airport, Paris in 2000 that put an end to supersonic passenger flights. The Concorde was uneconomic — it could not a carry enough passengers to make it pay — and it was so noisy that even countries like Malaysia banned it from flying over its airspace.

For the future — predicts Mr Lim — there will be supersonic passenger aircraft and they will be as quiet as today's passenger jets. They will have to be designed to carry at least 300 passengers a flight and they will offer the fastest and most convenient way to travel long distance for those who can afford to pay a premium.

A supersonic future is no pipedream. There are at least seven designs or concept plans in prospect.

Alex Davies in Business Insider set this out two years ago (September 2012) to show there's definitely a future for flying at supersonic heights. He points out that since the retirement of the Concorde jet travel hasn't become any faster.[13]

He sets out seven of the concept plans for supersonic aircraft, some are only renderings, others are already embarking on test flights. They all show that the future of travel is supersonic and it could well come from any of the following: Lockheed Martin, Japan's JAXA, Aerons in the US or EADS in Europe. Then there's the X-51 WaveRider, the combined work of DARPA, NASA, the Air Force, Boeing and Pratt & Whitney. Two other supersonic planes are on the drawing board: XCOR's Lynx and a Hypermach.

But before supersonic aircraft make their return, Mr Lim thinks we will be able to experience what the people in the Airbus survey wanted — more sustainable and eco-efficient aircraft. That is well on the way, with the design and manufacture of aircraft, along with the desire of the whole industry to reduce aviation's impact on the environment and cut its emissions of greenhouse gases.

When you see how far commercial aviation has come in 100 years — as Tony Tyler the Director General and CEO of IATA told an aviation conference in Singapore in February 2014 — you can start to think where it might be in the next 100 years. To him, the way forward for aviation involved improving regulation, ensuring sustainability and expanding connectivity[14]:

> *Our goals are to achieve a 1.5% improvement in fuel efficiency annually by 2020; to cap net emissions with carbon neutral growth from 2020 and cut net emissions in half by 2050 as compared to 2005 levels. And we will achieve this through a combination of four elements: better technology, infrastructure, operations, and with a global mechanism for market based measures (MBM).*

The same article went on to explain how a MBM scheme works and what is already happening on a voluntary basis, where according to IATA, at least 32 of its member airlines have introduced offset programmes, either integrated into their web-sales engines or to a third party offset provider.

Passengers can choose to offset the emissions caused by their flying. The principle is that emissions for each flight are divided amongst the passengers. Each passenger can therefore pay to offset the emissions caused by their share of the flight's emissions. The airlines then offset their emissions by investing in carbon reduction projects that generate carbon credits.

Market based schemes — even voluntary ones that airlines introduce — have the support of ICAO and IATA.

ICAO passed a resolution way back in 2010, which said, "Voluntary carbon offsetting schemes constitute a practical way to offset CO2 emissions, and invites States to encourage their operators wishing to take early actions to use carbon offsetting, particularly through the use of credits generated from internationally recognized schemes such as the CDM".

CDM is the Clean Development Mechanism (CDM), one of the flexibility mechanisms defined in the Kyoto Protocol (IPCC, 2007) that provides for emissions reduction projects which generate Certified Emission Reduction units which may be traded in emissions trading schemes. There are other recognised offset schemes that are also approved by IATA and other international organisations and NGOs (Non Government Organisations).

Market Based Mechanisms are only one way airlines plan to make future flights cleaner, with less impact on the environment.

While Mr Lim is the first to admit that there were not the same "environmental impact" pressures on airlines during his 30-odd years in the business. But in fact what SIA was doing for very good economic reasons in the 1980s and 1990s, by maintaining the most modern fleet in the world, had added benefits. The newer aircraft were more energy efficient than the ones they replaced. Less polluting, more productive, cleaner and greener than what went before.

SIA showed industry leadership then. To be ahead of the game. It did it then and it continues now.

The airline can proudly proclaim its commitment today to a more sustainable future tomorrow[15]:

- In August 2011, Singapore Airlines joined the Sustainable Aviation Fuel Users Group (SAFUG) to accelerate the development and commercialisation of lower-carbon renewable aviation fuels derived from environmentally and socially sustainable sources.
- Following a series of successful trial flights, Singapore Airlines has put into practice since November 2009 a new airline procedure for A380 operations at London's Heathrow Airport. This new procedure saves an additional 300kg of fuel per flight, which equates to almost one metric tonne of CO_2 emissions on a flight from London to Singapore.
- In February 2010, Singapore Airlines partnered aviation authorities in Singapore, the US and Japan to carry out the first multi-sector demonstration green flight under the Asia and Pacific Initiative to Reduce Emissions (ASPIRE) programme. As a result, it was able to use around 6 per cent less fuel than normally required for a similar flight.
- In May 2011, regular "green" flights across Asia and the Pacific were introduced through the ASPIRE programme. The non-stop flights between Los Angeles and Singapore reduced fuel burn and carbon emissions by some two tonnes per flight.

- Singapore Airlines says it will continue to be at the forefront of aviation's drive towards carbon-neutral growth with the aim of a sustainable future for the airline industry, supporting IATA's commitment for the industry to achieve carbon-neutral growth.

How do the big aircraft manufacturers see flying into the future? Airbus sees it this way[16].

In unveiling its 2050 vision for "Smarter Skies", Airbus allows for more flights, fewer emissions and quicker passenger journey times. For the first time, its vision for sustainable aviation in the future looks beyond aircraft design to how the aircraft is operated both on the ground and in the air in order to meet the expected growth in air travel in a sustainable way.

> *Already today, if the Air Traffic Management (ATM) system and technology on board aircraft were optimised (assuming around 30 million flights per year), Airbus research suggests that every flight in the world could on average be around 13 minutes shorter. This would save around 9 million tonnes of excess fuel annually, which equates to over 28 million tonnes of avoidable CO2 emissions and a saving for passengers of over 500 million hours of excess flight time on board an aircraft.*

The future, as Airbus see it, concentrates on operational achievements and the "Smarter Skies" vision, which consists of five concepts which could be implemented across all the stages of an aircraft's operation to reduce waste in the system (waste in time, waste in fuel, reduction of CO2). Its five include: eco-climb, express skyways, free glide approaches and landings, ground operations and power.

While Airbus makes a strong commitment to operational gains in the battle to make sure aviation maintains blue skies into the future, Boeing is making the most of its achievements in aircraft design and production. And still holds out its Dreamliner aircraft as its best contribution to date to the future of cleaner and clearer skies.

Boeing was described as "flying high in preparation" for the biggest airplane manufacturers' trade shows at Farnborough in July 2014 where the aircraft maker showed off its latest 787-9 Dreamliner, a key strategy in its competition with its main rival, Airbus. For its beginning ten years ago — in 2004 — Boeing wanted to make sure the 787 was better than anything before it[17].

"The key to the exceptional performance of the 787 Dreamliner is its suite of new technologies and its revolutionary design. Composite materials make up 50 percent of the primary structure of the 787, including the fuselage and wing".

Boeing insists that in addition to bringing big-jet ranges to midsize airplanes, the 787 family provides airlines with "unmatched fuel efficiency, resulting in exceptional environmental performance". The airplane uses 20% less fuel than today's similarly sized airplanes.

"Advances in engine technology are the biggest contributor to overall fuel efficiency improvements on the Dreamliner," Boeing states. The 787 features new engines from General Electric and Rolls-Royce that represent nearly a two-generation jump in technology.

In a report headlined "Battle for the future of the skies" in *The Guardian* in December 2013, Gwyn Topham drew attention[18] to the serious competition between Boeing and Airbus. She referred to its "troubled birth" but noted that Boeing's flagship 787 has overtaken the larger A380 in terms of orders. 'But can its fuel efficiency and range help it defeat its rival over the long haul?'

> *Topham points out that low fuel consumption and reduced noise have been the big selling points, but a key part of the 787's appeal to passengers is the increased cabin pressure said to alleviate the ill-effects of flying.*

The report continues by asking if the A380 is, as an Airbus spokesman put it, a "congestion buster", the 787 is better known as a "hub buster" — one that rewrites traditional models of funnelling connecting passengers onto the jumbos that make long-haul flying viable. With fewer seats, its fuel efficiency and range are enabling the likes of a direct Heathrow-Austin connection — BA's next new route for 2014 — even with less passenger demand than established routes.

The Guardian insists that on the simple comparison of orders, the 787 is beating the A380, though Airbus has the satisfaction of knowing its super-jumbo is slowly wiping the ageing Boeing 747 from the skies.

It is not just aircraft design and performance — even when it's better for the environment — that is so important to the passenger. As Mr Lim has noted, a determinant for the operation by airlines over long distances is how much "passengers can endure being cooped up in an aircraft".

So comfort and convenience will continue to be important for airline passengers in the future. In an article headed "Flying into the future" *The Economist* in 2013 looked at some beneficial innovations ahead.

It asked what a Silicon Valley entrepreneur would do to reinvent the industry and Jude Gomila, the co-founder of HeyZap, a gaming company offered some "off the wall" ideas. How about coating common surfaces with silver to prevent the spread of colds and flu? But frequent flyer Mr Gomila has put some serious thought into the issue[19].

He says airlines should learn from the shipping industry and re-engineer planes so that people are pre-loaded into detached air-conditioned cabins that would then be rolled onto the plane, thus allowing passengers to "board" before the plane even arrives.

The article also refers to *Reinventing the Airport Ecosystem*, by Amadeus which says, among other things, that by 2015 passengers should expect to see some of the industry's more forward-thinking members adopt measures such as passive "in-pocket" scanning of e-tickets and radio-frequency-ID-enabled travel documents, as well as near-field communication being used for "check-in, baggage check, security, boarding, lounge access and as a wallet, in and around the airport".

The Amadeus approach calls for seat allocation to be based on the amount of hand luggage a passenger is carrying. "The hope is that by 2025, passengers will be able to bypass the terminal entirely, with premium travellers checking in offsite and passing through security en-route. Biometric and perhaps even genetic information will be used to automatically check in passengers upon airport entry".

On board comfort is something that is needed at the back of the plane as it is on all low cost carriers, but very little effort has been put into designing a new economy class seat. Until now. This report from *Gizmag* about The AirGo Seat[20].

> *Flying economy class can be about as enjoyable as being stuffed into a left luggage locker, but Malaysia-based engineering student Alireza Yaghoubi has come up with a new economy class air passenger seat design that departs radically from the one that's been used since the 1960s. Winner of the Malaysian national James Dyson Award, the AirGo concept aims to make seats less expensive, easier to maintain and as comfortable as the leather and free drinks before take-off jobs up in first class.*

For AirGo, the seat consists of two parts. Above, there is an individual locker for each passenger which replaces conventional shared bins. Attached to this are a tray and touchscreen which are mounted independently on arms so they can be easily moved and configured or simply folded away when not wanted.

The AirGo seat itself consists of an articulated frame containing three motors that allow the passenger to customise its position. Instead of cushions, the back support has a nylon mesh that conforms to the body and prevents sweating. In addition, an integral part of the AirGo seat, is a footrest, rather than mounted on the seat in front.

Mr Lim would applaud such improvements which mean greater comfort for passengers on board, but he also wonders about how to satisfy those who want an even quieter and cleaner ride. Maybe the Solar Impulse is the aircraft of the future.

It is the work of two men who are pioneers, innovators and pilots. The driving force behind Solar Impulse is Bertrand Piccard, doctor, psychiatrist, explorer and aeronaut. He made the first non-stop round-the-world balloon flight and is the project initiator and chairman. André Borschberg, an engineer and graduate in management science, a fighter pilot — a professional airplane and helicopter pilot — is the co-founder and CEO[21].

Together they are attempting to rewrite the next pages in aviation history with solar energy, and voyaging around the world without fuel or pollution. Their ambition is for the world of exploration and innovation to contribute to the cause of renewable energies, to demonstrate the importance of clean technologies for sustainable development; and to place dreams and emotions back at the heart of scientific adventure.

The Solar Impulse is not the first solar airplane ever designed, but it is certainly the most ambitious. None of its predecessors has ever managed to fly right through the night.

The flying inventors admit they are "dealing here with a symbol, as solar airplanes are unlikely ever to carry 300 passengers, but it is a symbol that affects all of us. In fact, aren't we all on Earth in the same situation as the Solar Impulse pilot?"

They ask the eternal question: If man does not have the right technologies or wastes his energy, he will have to land before the rising sun enables him to continue his flight. "And as for us, if we do not invest in the scientific means to develop new energy sources, we shall find ourselves in a major crisis, which will prevent us from handing over the planet to the next generation".

So is the future of flight a solar powered plane which can transverse the earth without using one litre of fuel, except for that freely provided by the sun?

Or does it mean going "back to the future" with quieter but powerful supersonic passenger jets or maybe a "voyage in a ship" that takes us beyond earth to the edge of space?

There's no doubt in Lim Chin Beng's mind that people will want to fly in ever increasing numbers to even more places. The Airbus survey bears that out, just as it shows a desire for a more sustainable, less stressful air travel experience.

Flying in the future presents a dilemma and a challenge for those in the aviation industry responsible for producing the machines and making them fly. How to do that, bearing in mind not only the dreams and demands of people, but to do it for the planet and for profit?

There's at least one man who has played his part — many parts in fact — in delivering flying pleasure to millions around the world.

For the man they still call "Mr SIA", the letter "S" must figure prominently on the passport when flying into the future: Supersonic, safe, secure, sustainable, space, solar, and silent.

But the capital "S" word which Lim Chin Beng counts on to continue to provide leadership in the future of aviation is none other than the place which has figured so prominently in the fly past over the first 100 years of commercial aviation... Singapore.

Endnotes

1. Airbus survey for the future, innovations and a concept plane is available at http://www.airbus.com/innovation/future-by-airbus/.

2. On China's largest outbound tourist market, see UNWTO Press Release (20 January 2014) at http://media.unwto.org/press-release/2014-01-20/international-tourism-exceeds-expectations-arrivals-52-million-2013.

3. For the numbers on Chinese tourists, see http://www.travelchinaguide.com/tourism/.

4. A showcase for airports of the future at the World Airport Expo (held annually), more information can be found at http://worldairportexpo.com.sg/about-wae.

5. For more information on the SIA cargo subsidiary, see its official website at http://www.siacargo.com/.

6. "Project Wing: Google's plans for drone-based deliveries, aid efforts revealed" by Alexei Oreskovic (1 September 2014), *Reuters*. Available at http://uk.reuters.com/article/2014/09/01/uk-google-drones-idUKKBN0GS2QZ20140901.

7. Report from *New York Times* by Mark Scott on 25 September 2014 entitled "DHL to begin deliveries by drone in Germany".

8. From speech given by Lim Chin Beng to MBA Students from the University of Texas, visiting Singapore in January 2005. From Mr Lim's personal archives.

9. On Branson's Virgin Galactic space flight go ahead, see http://www.dailymail.co.uk/sciencetech/article-2642917/Virgin-FAA-sign-agreement-Spaceport-flights.html

10. "We can send humans back to space ... if we fund Elon Musk instead of NASA" by Joe Pappalardo (26 June 2014), *The Guardian*. Available at http://www.theguardian.com/commentisfree/2014/jun/26/space-nasa-into-elon-musk-vc-fund-private-space-industry.

11. "Ticket sales for commercial space flights launched in Singapore" by Faris Mokhtar (29 August 2014), *Channel News Asia*. Available at http://www.channelnewsasia.com/news/singapore/ticket-sales-for/1336180.html.

12. From speech by Lim Chin Beng to MBA Students from the University of Texas.

13. Read more on the concepts for supersonic aircraft of the future at http://www.businessinsider.com/the-future-of-supersonic-flight-2012-8?op=1#ixzz3BmkUazP5

14. Tony Tyler was quoted in this article by the author summing up the discussions at the associated Singapore Airshow conference and covering plans to deal with carbon emissions from the aviation industry. It also published online by Ana Shell Media, available at http://anashell.com/anashell/2014/03/11/blue-skies-ahead-greener-flights/.

15. Singapore Airlines update on its sustainability practices can be found at http://www.singaporeair.com/en_UK/about-us/sia-history/sia-environment/.

16. How Airbus sees the future of flying can be read at http://www.airbus.com/innovation/future-by-airbus/.

17. About Boeing and its 787 Dreamliner is available at http://www.boeing.com/boeing/commercial/787family/background.page.

18. "Battle for the future of the skies: Boeing 787 Dreamliner v Airbus A380" by Gwyn Topham (29 December 2013), *The Guardian*. Available at http://www.theguardian.com/business/2013/dec/29/boeing-787-dreamliner-airbus-a380-battle-for-skies.

19. Innovations for passengers from *The Economist*, found at http://www.economist.com/blogs/gulliver/2013/03/end-of-check-in-airlines.

20. "AirGo seat concept aims to up the comfort in coach class" by David Szondy (20 February 2013), *Gizmag*. Available at http://www.gizmag.com/airgo-economy-seat-concept/26339/. The author has also met the designers of AirGo and seen the designs first hard.

21. The Solar Impulse story is available on the official website at http://www.solarimpulse.com/en/our-story/change-the-world/#.VAO2j8WSya8.

"DEVIL'S ADVOCATE"

It all started when I met up with Lim Chin Beng and his son Arthur at the Shangri-La Hotel in Orange Grove Road in April 2013. Sadly, his dear wife Winnie had died the month before. Besides sharing reminisces about her and our past times together, he proudly told me that he had finally retired from all his jobs: his directorships and what he called his "national service". I ventured that now he would have time to write his memoirs. He immediately dismissed that idea, so I quickly got in and offered to write them for him. He agreed.

So during the rest of 2013 and the first few months of 2014, I spent many delightful hours meeting with him — he was happy to be called Chin Beng but I often still addressed him as Mr Lim — and gathering archives, photographs, old speech notes and anything I could lay my hands on about the man and his work. While I took notes — and once or twice recorded an "interview" — it was always more like a fireside chat, without the fire. Most times we met in his apartment on Orange Grove Road, just along from the Shangri-La. Most times Arthur was around too and willingly chipped in with contributions and helped hunt out photos, dates and old files.

Our conversations covered his many years in the airline business, first Malayan Airways, Malaysian Airways, Malaysia-Singapore Airlines and Singapore Airlines (SIA). And of course his venture into the low cost carrier business with Valuair, which also involved Arthur and other people I knew quite well. Before that, something of his early days: school, university, music and sport. His early days in government service and the many times since when he was called back for important work. And of course his time in Japan as Ambassador and his many other business experiences.

But my very first meeting with Mr Lim was, in fact, many years' previous — in October 1983 to be exact — when I was a public affairs consultant to the airline. I remember quite clearly the first session I had with him in his impressive Deputy Chairman's office at the relatively new Airline House at Changi Airport.

We discussed a lot of things in that first briefing but I recall vividly his words to me. He wanted me to be a "devil's advocate". A strange request? On reflection, quite normal coming from this man. I think he had checked me out in advance and was aware that I had some involvement in the airline business and in the media.

As I understood it, I was to be involved in helping to understand SIA's position in expanding its services around the world, in its "international relations" and traffic rights issues, in explaining the need for greater air liberalisation — freedom of the skies — and in getting across to all who would read or listen to the views of this enterprising airline from a small country which was thinking big.

I was also to write position papers and assist with speaking opportunities and speeches for the airline's Chairman and Deputy Chairman. A couple of days earlier, I had met with Mr Pillay in Hong Kong where he was speaking to a chamber of commerce meeting and I attended a media briefing with him.

Of course, I was happy to be a "devil's advocate", which I took to mean he wanted me to test the waters, to open doors where they might be closed — particularly with the foreign media — to point out where things could be said and done better. To also keep my ear to the ground, to report back and to point out where a particular approach was required or where it might not always work, or where some behind the scenes activity might be considered.

A tall order may be, but one which would involve working closely with Mr Lim and his senior people, and it involved a lot of travel. In the course of this, I got to know the man and his mission. I also worked with him at the Singapore Tourist Promotion Board — as it was called then — when he was Chairman, so that gave me additional opportunities to deal with him regarding speeches, events, media and the like.

We have kept in touch over the years, even when I was in Australia (2000–2010). Email exchanges, Christmas cards and catching up when I came on visits to Singapore. But I have kept at least one gem from our occasional correspondence. It was a Singapore Technologies Engineering official "season's greetings" card he sent to me when he was Chairman of ST Aerospace. Among the words, in his own hand-writing inside the card, were these:

> *I have also been asked to do more national service and am now Chairman of Singapore Press Holdings. Hope to be able to visit you in the near future.*
>
> *Winnie and Chin Beng*

Typical of the man they called the "quiet achiever". Understatement and modesty rolled into one. We seemed to have this running joke about "national service". He never did the physical National Service in Singapore, but he well and truly made up for that by giving his life and times to the country and its important institutions — public and private.

As Singapore approaches its 50th anniversary in 2015, it is a good time to stop and think about the men and women who have contributed so much and maybe, in some cases, not been given all the recognition they deserve.

Lim Chin Beng has just got on with his "national service" in his own quiet and effective way. His story deserves to be told and it has been a pleasure to spend time with such a true gentlemen and friend, to delve into and share his story with readers far and wide.

There are many things I hope the reader will get from this book — whether they feel that they know the man well or not. I hope, more than anything, that the reader can see he was in fact much more than "Mr SIA" and more than a "legend in international aviation".

He was a visionary. He was a very articulate thinker. He has urged Singaporeans to have "an appreciation for the arts, music, sports, foreign cultures, current events worldwide and in the region, networking skills, social graces and even learning to play golf".

He wanted Singapore to be "a truly global city, pulsating with cultural, social, political and economic vigour". He hoped (when he said this in 2001) that

Singapore can "produce world class sportsmen/women, musicians, painters, artists, writers, philosophers".

He is one "foreign-born" Singaporean who has become one of the best examples of citizenship and leadership, who is so totally committed to doing his best for the country and its people. A specialist and a generalist. An arts and sports lover. A businessman with his heart and mind in the right place. A people person. A man who has taken the best the world can offer and combined it with home-grown talent, determination, risk-taking and entrepreneurial spirit. With all this he has been instrumental in creating not only a world class airline but also contributed, more than most, to making Singapore a truly global city.

Ken Hickson
October 2014

BIBLIOGRAPHY

A selection of books the author read, referenced and/or wrote — and recommends — which have some relevance to the subject of the biography, Lim Chin Beng, or related subjects covered in this book:

Allen, Roy (1990). *SIA: Take off to Success,* Singapore Airlines.

Batey, Ian (2002). *Asian Branding: A Great Way to Fly,* Prentice Hall.

Branson, Richard (1998). *Losing My Virginity,* Random House.

De Botton, Alain (2003). *The Art of Travel,* Penguin.

Dunnaway, Cliff (ed.) (1998). *Wings Over Hong Kong,* Odyssey.

Goh, Yong Kiat (2012). *Where Lions Fly,* Straits Times Press.

Heracleous, Loizos, Wirtz, Jochen and Pangarkar, Nitan (2009). *Flying High in a Competitive Industry,* McGraw-Hill.

Hickson, Ken (1980). *Flight 901 to Erebus,* Whitcoulls.

——————— (2009). *The ABC of Carbon,* ABC Carbon.

——————— (2013), *Race for Sustainability,* World Scientific.

Hudson, Kenneth and Pettifer, Julian (1979), *Diamonds in the Sky,* Bodley Head.

Hutton, Peter (1981). *Wings over Singapore,* MPH.

Koh, Tommy and Chang, Li Lin (2005). *The Little Red Dot: Reflections by Singapore's Diplomats,* World Scientific.

Macnamara, Jim (1992). *Asia Pacific Public Relations Handbook,* Archipelago Press.

Tan, Guan Heng (2007). *100 Inspiring Rafflesians,* World Scientific.

Young, Gavin (1988). *Beyond Lion Rock,* Hutchinson.

ACKNOWLEDGMENTS

D on't let anyone tell you are writing a book, particularly a biography, is a lonely existence where you are locked away on your own without any contact with the real world. Yes, of course there are the many hours (days and nights) when one is cooped up with the keyboard, pounding out wise and wonderful words, but in equal measure there's contact with people everywhere — in person, by email, by telephone, in conference calls and attending relevant events.

Spending time with Lim Chin Beng has been a particular pleasure in the process. He and son Arthur have been very forthcoming with words and pictures — anecdotes and archives — and I thank them both for the fruitful time and consideration they've given me. But I found that in the historical and biographical search for relevance and credibility, it is vital to search and source beyond the obvious subject of the book.

Many others have been very helpful in so many ways, but mostly by offering up photographs and related gems of information, long forgotten, even buried but not lost forever. This book will be sharing many images and items which have never seen the light of day — at least not for many a year.

Much appreciation, therefore, to the following people and institutions:

— **National Archives, Oral History Centre**, Singapore where I found such a wealth of information on and by Mr Lim. I was given access to and was able to use pieces of a very enlightening interview conducted by Patricia Lee in the year 2000. There were also many photographs there to look at even though permission to use was not automatic. Other original sources had to be contacted for approval.

— **Singapore Airlines** has been particularly helpful and while I stress this is not an official, approved airline history — it is "his story" built around the personality and life of Mr Lim — I have to thank Nick Ionides, Wilson Heng, Irene Manuel and Chua Xiao Ying for their approval to use many photos from the airline archives. Photos are suitably credited where they appear in the book. Wilson has been such an enthusiastic retriever and supplier of hidden gems — including a management memo from 1971 when Mr Lim was appointed first Deputy Managing Director, then Managing Director of MSA — that he should be appointed the "official airline archivist"!

— **Singapore Press Holdings** for giving access to their vast photo library and thanks to Malcolm McLeod, in particular, for the very helpful introduction. Straits Times Editor Patrick Daniel graciously permitted us to freely use a number of photos as this is "a special case, as Lim Chin Beng was our former chairman". So thanks also to Chin Soo Fang, Head Corporate Communications & CSR, as well as the kind people in the SPH photo library.

— **Raffles Institution**, fondly remembered the young Lim Chin Beng (a student from 1948 to 1951), and even came up with a genuine Leaving Certificate for the young man and a couple of sports team photographs, one of which we have used for chapter 2. Thanks to Cheryl Yap, Head, Archives & Museum at Raffles Institution.

— **Ascott and CapitaLand** people have been very helpful, particularly in identifying and allowing us to use the great shot of Mr Lim for the cover, as well as providing us with the chapter 22 photo we wanted. Thanks to Joan Tan, Anthony Khoo and Susanna Ong.

— **Experia Events** has been very helpful with archival material from airshows past and present, including memorable photographs and the text of Mr Lim's 2008 "show stopper" speech. Thanks to Leck Chet Lam and Lloyd Tan.

— **Changi Airport Group** has done the airport proud by keeping such a good record of the early days of Changi's development and since by recording the role of its important players, including Mr Lim. We have, I think, made good use of the material and we give Changi all the recognition it deserves as the world's leading airport.

— **Singapore Tourism Board** and its Chairman Chew Choon Seng has been very encouraging, also providing a welcome additional Foreword, and STB staff, in particular Pauline Low, have also been helpful sourcing for archival photos and publications of significant times in its past when Mr Lim figured prominently.

— **Starhub** makes an appearance in the book as Mr Lim was a director of the telecoms company for 12 years. He speaks highly of the organisation and vice versa. We also quote liberally from the company's philosophy and practice of corporate social responsibility and thank Jeannie Ong for being helpful over the years.

Many other individuals have been very helpful in different ways, by providing support, information, access to material, including photos and giving me the benefit of their knowledge and recollections, particularly where they knew and worked with Mr Lim:

— **Chai Hon Yam**, Project Manager for many years at SIA (and its predecessor airlines) who spent a lot of time with me going through the evaluation process before the airline committed to buy its first jumbo jets. He has written a book about his work and airline's meticulous engineered selection process. It deserves to be published.

— **Ian Batey** did some sterling work for the airline, which Mr Lim duly acknowledges and so do I. We have some pertinent quotes from his book "Asian Branding" and one of the SIA ads from the Batey Ads days.

— **Aiden O'Rourke**, willingly allowed me to use a great airline tail line-up at Manchester Airport, which he took in 1998, which perfectly illustrates Chapter 11. Thanks from Singapore to Manchester.

— **Jim Macnamara**, an old friend and collaborator in my former PR days, refreshed my memory of the Manchester campaign with an extract from his book *Asia Pacific Public Relations Handbook*.

Authors, writers and fellow journalists do rely on the collective and individual strengths of each other, and I have to admit I had no hesitation in drawing on the work of fellow scribes, with due acknowledgement of course. Every reference to the work and writings of others are duly noted in the chapter and the endnotes at the conclusion of every chapter. Some also appear in the selective bibliography of books.

I do want to make special note of some of these people who I know and who have contributed some choice pieces to this biographical work:

— **Michael Richardson**, formerly *International Herald Tribute* and a great foreign correspondent based in Singapore for many years. He now contributes irregular articles to the Straits Times in his capacity as a fellow of the Institute of South East Asian Studies.

— **Karamjit Kaur**, who does such a good job as *Straits Times* aviation correspondent, has been faithfully and judiciously reporting the scene so well for many years. I have dipped into a lot of her reports, particularly from the Valuair days when Mr Lim was the news.

— **Steven Howard**, an old friend who knows Singapore, the airline and its leaders well, for his encouragement, insight and a quote or two from his collection 'Asian Words of Wisdom'.

— **Hugh McAtear**, for his work on Flight Show Dailies over many years, as well as a very perceptive and useful interview with Mr Lim a few years back.

While their books appear in the Bibliography, I do want to make special note of those who have diligently and faithfully recorded some of Singapore's very notable history:

Roy Allen's 1990 book *SIA: Take off to Success*; **Goh Yong Kiat's** *Where Lions Fly*; **Peter Hutton's** *Wings over Singapore*; **Tan Guan Heng's** *100 Inspiring Rafflesians* and the wonderful *Little Red Dot*, the diplomatic collection brought together by Professor **Tommy Koh** and **Chang Li Lin**. There's also the work by three academics, **Loizos Heracleous, Jochen Wirtz** and **Nitan Pangarkar**, called *Flying High in a Competitive Industry* which was a very thorough attempt to put SIA's service philosophy into words and well worth while studying.

A few others gave a lot of their time — often under pressure — to share their knowledge of, and experience working with, Mr Lim. One of note is **Jimmy Lau**, who not only worked with our biographical "hero" at Asian Aerospace and Singapore Airshow, but also joined forces with him to help bring about the land-mark launch of Valuair, as Singapore first approved "budget" airline. Thanks Jimmy! I have known him and worked with him myself over the years and know what a tireless worker and inspired leader he is.

We have drawn on the resources and archives of many other organisations, like **Boeing, Airbus, Balmain** and **Landor**, as they had, whether they knew it or not, a significant contribution to make to the airline and to story of "Mr SIA".

I also have to make a very special thanks to **JY Pillay**, the father of Singapore Airlines, who wrote such a thoughtful and generous Foreword for the book, which was provided — as only Mr Pillay could say — with such "alacrity". His selection of words and his genuine acknowledgement of the role Lim Chin Beng played as "a key personality in the making of an outstanding airline", demonstrated Mr Pillay's knowledge of, and genuine friendship with, "a trusted colleague" over many decades.

On a more personal, but also professional level, I must thank the Australian-based artist **Dave Hickson** — who also happens to be my son — for contributing a delightful artistic impression to illustrate Chapter 5, appropriately entitled "Tall on Talent". I have to admit I have taken advantage of my son's talent before to illustrate my books. This is the third time.

Personally, I also need to acknowledge the role my dear wife **M Hickson** plays — largely behind the scenes — and who has had to endure (and feed and clothe) this author who insists on doing most of his labour at his "home office" for the sixth book now. Hers is a "labour of love", even when she agrees to do some proof-reading, and she is much appreciated for her support and attention to detail.

World Scientific have once again agreed to be my publishers and they have tackled this book with enthusiasm and professionalism. Thanks to **Max Phua** for taking me on board and for having very capable people like **Lee Xin Ying** (until February this year) and others, as editors, designers and typesetters, who have had to put up with the wily ways of this writer!

Ken Hickson
October 2014

ABOUT THE AUTHOR

With in-depth experience in the airline industry and as a former aviation journalist, Ken Hickson is in an ideal position to produce this biography *Mr SIA: Fly Past*. He also worked as a consultant to Singapore Airlines and the Singapore Tourist Promotion Board between 1983 and 1990.

Before this latest book, Ken authored five non-fiction works: *Flight 901 to Erebus* (a documentary account of an aviation disaster in the Antarctic), *The Future South, Forty: Building a Future in Singapore*, *The ABC of Carbon* and *Race for Sustainability*.

He started his working life as a journalist in New Zealand, working for newspapers, radio, television and magazines. He was the editor of the aviation safety magazine *Topic Air* and also contributed to many other aviation and travel magazines.

Working in national news and current affairs for South Pacific Television and Television New Zealand, Ken was for a time the network's aviation/airline industry correspondent. He also worked on the educational programme "Science Express" as reporter/presenter, which included spending a month in the Antarctic researching and reporting science news. For two and a half years, he worked for Air Zealand in a public relations position based in Auckland, also handling assignments in the Pacific Islands and Australia.

He first visited Singapore in 1981, the year Changi Airport opened and he attended the first Asian Aerospace at Paya Lebar airport.

He came to live in Singapore in October 1983 to work as a public affairs consultant for Singapore Airlines.

In 1986, he set up a communications consultancy to co-ordinate and manage international and regional programmes for the Singapore Tourist Promotion Board, then for other clients including DHL, BMW, Intel, Lend Lease, Hitachi and Canon, as well as for other members of the Star Alliance, United Airlines and Lufthansa.

His consultancy also acted for the Civil Aviation Authority of Singapore (CAAS) between 1995–98, covering the opening of the new air traffic control centre and promoting Changi Airport, including an "Ideas Contest" for the Third Terminal. He has managed media relations for major events, including Asian Aerospace Forum (Singapore), APEC Forum (Manila), Miss Universe Pageant (Singapore) Asia Travel Market and PATA (Pacific Asia Travel Association).

In mid-1990s, Hickson PR was acquired by Fleishman Hillard and he moved to Australia at the end of 2000 for ten years. He was in demand as a consultant, writer and lecturer, and was appointed as an adjunct associate professor at the University of the Sunshine Coast. He started *ABC Carbon* as a consultancy and publishing business in 2007, producing *The ABC of Carbon* as a print and e-book, and started the e-newsletter *abc carbon express*.

He returned to Singapore in September 2010 to establish his consultancy Sustain Ability Showcase Asia (SASA) and a year later acquired a communications consultancy which he re-branded H2PC Asia. He and his team have worked for many clients, including Armstrong Asset Management, The Blue Circle, International Energy Centre, Serious Games International, Singapore Road Safety Council, Third Wave Power, and the National Environment Agency (NEA).

His company was appointed sustainability consultant for Asia's first and only sustainable light art festival — i Light Marina Bay — presented by the Urban Redevelopment Authority (URA) in March 2012 and again in March 2014, managing an associated energy efficiency programme, "Switch Off, Turn Up" campaign.

Ken has been associated with the World Wide Fund for Nature over many years, acting as its honorary representative in Singapore in the 1990s and appointed a Governor of WWF Australia.

He is often invited to be a speaker and/or moderator at conferences and events in Singapore and the region. In 2013 and 2014 he has actively participated in international conferences in Taiwan, Malaysia and Japan, as well as many in Singapore, including the Green Growth and Business Forum (June 2014), when he was session and conference chairman.

He is also Regional Director Asia for the international consulting group, Be Sustainable and Singapore chairman of the International Green Purchasing Network.

Ken and his artist wife M Hickson have lived in Singapore for a total of 21 Years.